WHERE THE STREETS HAVE NO NAME

A GUIDE TO HOMING STREET DOGS

M. CONNOR

🐦 @iamselfpub
www.iamselfpublishing.com

Dedicated to dogs everywhere.
Lost and found, homed and homeless, near and far, those
here with us and those rainbow bridge travelers.

*'When the world around me is going crazy, and I am losing
faith in humanity, I just have to take one look at my dog
and I know, good still exists'*. Anon

CONTENTS

INTRODUCTION

The age old battle of cat person or dog person is not something I have ever had any trouble with. Moreover, I have merely found that despite my mix of experiences with both, they were both always close to my heart at various stages of my life and will continue to be so for many years to come. In my very early years however, I was absolutely in love with dogs and found my heart stolen by a gorgeous Border collie pup called 'Shep'. Ok, sounds like a cliché name but it suited him and evolved lovingly into 'Sheppie-poos', which he seemed to really like. Hey, I was all of about seven years old, it seemed like a good name at the time. Despite the enormous difficulty of trying to walk and train him, which I felt was my responsibility, my futile efforts to do so had not so much trained or exercised him but built what I felt to be an unbreakable bond that would see us together forever. For a seven year old, forever is a long time, and it really is forever! He was my life and my best friend. Little did I realise that my parents were making arrangements to rehome him due to our lack of experience with dogs and, in particular, this rather intelligent and somewhat busy breed. Not only that, as a single parent household, the expense of owning a dog became overwhelming for my mother. She had to make a decision between feeding us properly or him. It absolutely broke my heart when I discovered he was no longer there. No words could console me and I cried and sobbed for weeks after, eventually coming to terms with it and having never forgotten him. I've always lived with cats (and still do), having owned no less than four of my own at one time (all rescues) and filling the void left when they passed on with other rescue cats, always the ones that no one wanted, and the ones labelled as 'trouble' (I have a soft spot for naughty torties!). Fast forward twenty years and there I was with a child of my own. I felt it was the right time for a puppy. Ignorant and driven to make my daughter's dreams come true, and secretly my own, I scoured the papers and found an advert for Border Collie puppies. Remembering the experience of Shep and convinced that, being older and wiser, I was in a good position to understand this breed as I had understood him all those years ago. I went right ahead and made the call. Sickeningly, I later realised having read an article in a magazine that the set up I had bought from was a puppy farm. I felt awful, desperately sad for his siblings and more than that, his poor mother. Determined to not let him down, I vowed I would make his life happy. This young, spritely chap stayed with us for just six short months. He ate through walls, telephone cables and carpets. He was incredibly loving but so demanding of exercise and time. Living in rented accommodation at the time, and having spent those months getting to know the wants and needs of this little chap, I felt he would be better suited to an area where there was a lot of space and someone experienced with this breed. History repeated itself with my heart breaking over this gorgeous black and white bundle of pure love, but this time gaining a valuable lesson in responsibility and ending in a situation better suited to his exuberant nature, allowing him to blossom and shine. He went to a lovely fruit farm owner with acres and acres of land. The farmer was so lovely and invited us to visit him until we were ready to really let go and see him settle in. We knew we did absolutely the right thing for him after our first visit, but it was hard to let go. By our third visit, we decided it really was time to let him go and leave him to enjoy his new life and he was truly, undeniably happy. I realised right there and then that, despite my fondness for dogs, perhaps I was not the right person for a dog and vowed I would never take on another.

Life has a funny way of catching up with you, and unbelievably, another life lesson that came in the form of a broken soul whose details were posted on social media. The lesson this time was never say 'Never'. There I was in the latter part of 2012 toying with the idea of getting a dog due to this void I felt inside. I hadn't forgotten my previous experiences with dogs and as much as I wanted one, I had some reservations. If, as an animal lover you've ever had the gut-wrenching experience letting go of an animal you adore, I'm sure you'll know exactly what I'm referring to. It really does hurt so much when you have to say goodbye, no matter how justified the reasons. But here I was, with all this in the balance and still considering the possibilities. Then, one grey and dismal morning, the universe presented me with a Facebook experience that would change our whole house dynamic and our lives completely.

The decision to get a dog is initially all about the self, but to fully take on a rescue animal, especially one from a far off land, who you haven't had the opportunity to meet and know little to nothing about, takes great courage and commitment. However, there are covenants, things that you may not be aware of and things that really aren't discussed in enough detail to potential families of these dogs prior to adoption. This is not a criticism of those who work in street dog rescue, more an observation based on my own experience, as is all any of us can do. In reading forums and social media and discovering that many others were having the same problems as we were having with our rescue, it quickly became apparent that there are behaviours that these dogs pick up by the natural process of filial imprinting (behaviours learned quickly during the sensitive phase of the pup's life) and latent learning (behaviours picked up by example and carried on by association). I wonder if rescuers and charities of foreign street dogs are so familiar with these unique characteristics and behaviours that they now see street dog behaviour as 'normal' and overlook passing on information about potential issues when offering a dog up for homing?

In my humble opinion, having overcome the unexpected difficulties with my own street dog rescues, of which not all were entirely happy endings for us humans, I feel that more information could be made available for potential owners or those who have already committed and need some support and have no idea where to turn. Moreover, there are those that feel that they can't ask for help for whatever reason. If you have a dog, regardless of whether it's a foreign rescue or not, and feel out of your depth, please know there is <u>never</u> any shame in asking for help and support. Asking for help does not always mean losing an animal you love, but it does mean finding the best solution that works for the welfare of the dog and your sanity. There are people who can help and each situation is unique. No-one understands your situation better than you. Unless you make contact and share those animal related issues with someone who can help, the situation will continue to spiral out of control which is extremely upsetting all round. So please take heart and don't hesitate to contact someone who can help. You are not alone. Please check out the resources at the back of this book.

The fact of the matter is, when it comes to street dogs, there is very little information available. Even scientific research is limited, yet street dog rescue continues to grow in popularity. More often than not when I take my dogs out, I'll meet up with a dog walker who shares the origin of his or her beloved poochie.

And so we lead nicely into the purpose of this book. I don't claim to be an expert, but, much like my hero Albert Einstein, 'I am passionately curious' with a wealth of experience as the owner of two non-UK rescue dogs, and a further two unsuccessful rescues to some degree, which I'd like to share with you. I've always had a passion for understanding animal behavior and continue to grow my knowledge with CPD (continued professional development) courses. This interest in animal behaviour fascinated me during my time at University, introducing me to texts from experts such as Professor Marc Beckoff of Colorado University, USA. His significant work for me was, 'The Emotional Lives of Animals' which comes highly recommended. I studied at degree level in Conservation and Biology with Greenwich University before transferring to Canterbury Christ Church University to continue my studies in Conservation and Ecology for which I now hold a full degree with honours. A large part of my studies for my degree covered not simply the hard sciences of biology, physics and chemistry, but also animal behavior, breeding and genetics. So join me as I debunk some of the misconceptions, do away with some rather bonkers assumptions, and basically just give potential rescuers a clearer picture of what they are taking on. I promise not to bamboozle you with scientific jargon and hope you gain some valuable insight from my efforts to educate.

CHAPTER 1
'WHAT BREED IS THE DOG?'

People seem to have always been obsessed with particular dog breeds, although when I was growing up, it was quite common for people to own mongrels. Although perhaps this perspective has more to do with the area I grew up in?! However, it has become increasingly obvious with the opportunities given by social media and other technological advances in the last decade or so that people have become more obsessed with particular dog breeds. Breeds such as Pugs, Dachshunds and French Bull Dogs have nigh-on quadrupled in value and popularity. There are even YouTube channels dedicated to these dogs. Many of these dogs have become celebrities themselves! Tea cup dogs, Chihuahuas, and other handbag-sized breeds are also in high demand and have remained so throughout the last thirty years plus. Devout Chihuahua owners might even boast this breed as being the original celebrity pooch. Adorable as all these dogs are, it's as though we have been conditioned by the constant media attention of these breeds and celebrity that to have value, there must be a label, a pigeon-hole, a box in order for us to make our choices and judgements on and about them. It's as though people have lost the ability to accept and appreciate the beauty of anything without its respective label. It's as if the label gives value by default. But ask anyone who's rescued a run-of-the-mill scruffy dog, a Heinz 57, a crossbreed (call it what you will, they all amount to the same), a street dog from a far off land

and they will tell you that once you see past the uniqueness of the baggage they come with and the perspective you see them through based on your own experiences throughout life, there is a just another loving soul full of joy and wonder waiting to embrace life with you.

The much acclaimed Czech scientist and father of genetics Gregor Mendel researched tirelessly the study of heredity by carrying out experiments using pea plants. Referred to now as the 'laws of Mendelian Inheritance' he showed that by selecting particular plants with dominant traits, he could predict the traits of the next generation of pea plants. This oversimplification does not do his work justice, but for the purposes of this book and the introduction of 'breeds' it is enough. For over a century, the aristocracy has used this law and applied it to perfect what we now know as 'pedigrees'. While these aesthetically pleasing dogs may melt your heart, the trade-off for them has meant health complications that range from minor discomfort to life threatening conditions. Many require surgery at some point in their lives in an attempt to ease the discomfort and serious health issues they live with. For others this has meant reduced longevity. I personally find it hard to justify the welfare and ethics of this practice, regardless of how adorable they look. Selective breeding is often sought in order to determine not only aesthetics but temperament of the dog. Having said that, I have been bitten three times in my life, each time was by the jaws of a pedigree. Perhaps this was the result of something I did or did not do? Regardless, I guess all dogs have bad days, regardless of social status and standing.

For street dogs, there are also trade-offs, some are health related due to the environments in which they live, some may be genetic although this is much reduced given the scale of breeding. No two litters are the same. However, the biggest trade-off is the misconception about them. We have been so conditioned by the media that many assume them to be savage, opportunistic, ruthless, wily street urchins. To some degree, part of that judgement is correct. They are indeed wily (they've always had to be), they can be opportunistic (I'll discuss in more detail in 'behaviour') and they are street urchins, but in my experience, I have never met a savage or ruthless street dog and never heard of anyone else encountering such an experience. Every single foreign dog I have ever met has been the sweetest, kindest, friendliest pooch. They just adore the love and attention of humans. That, in part is probably also down to being the very nature of dogs. The very nature of humans though, appears to have been somewhat diluted over the short time we've been here on this beautiful, miraculous planet.

Having written two wonderful short poem picture books of my two gorgeous rescues, I set about enlisting the help of a creative and masterful illustrator to complement my work. After giving what I believed to be a good account of my vision of the completed books, the cover, the lay-out and feel of the images I envisaged, the medium I saw the images displayed in etc. I courteously attached an image of one of my dogs to each email I sent telling prospective illustrators that they would need to apply their craft to emphasise the feeling and intent of each image to the reader. I felt I'd given them plenty to go on, with room for them to apply their own particular style. The image was of my first rescue, a little brown dog. Here in this image was a pathetic, scrawny, hopeless soul whose ribs were easily visible; a desperate soul who had clearly all but given up on life. When I first saw this image myself, it broke my heart. It was my gut response that told me I had to get her out of that situation. It didn't matter what breed she was, her location, how old she was, or even how big she would get. I just knew I had to get her out. So throwing caution to the wind, I set about making contact with a charity and then making arrangements to bring her to the UK to begin her life with us, surrounded by love, trust and respect. It mattered only that she would be able to start her journey to repair herself internally, to build her confidence, her sense of self-worth and experience the joy that is her birthright every day and in every way imaginable.

After the initial email to each potential illustrator, I was totally surprised when each responded, without pause or hesitation, with practically the same email, all asking the following question, 'what breed is the dog?'. I was perplexed by the need to know this information. I mean, I didn't even know 'what breed' myself, nor did I actually care. What mattered to me was that this gorgeous little soul had a home, felt an abundance of love and security every day, and was finally free from the atrocities she'd lived through in the first months of her life. So why did they need to know what breed she was? The work I had put together for them told them everything they needed to know, that I'd written two books about rescue dogs, with a poetic theme, that they would need to apply their craft to emphasise the feeling of the imagery. I even offered to supply images throughout the process of various situations that the dogs would have been subjected to. But still, the only question they wanted answered is 'what breed is the dog?'

I didn't for one moment consider that they were breed-specific illustrators, that they were, perhaps, prejudice towards the dog in some way, shape or form. However, on reflection, for what other reason would one need to know the breed of any animal if they were just going to be reproducing the image of it? When looking at the image of a cat, we rarely consider what breed it is, unless we can clearly see there is definite colouration or patterning not seen in a regular domestic shorthaired cat, or perhaps the shape of the face, ears or some other physical feature is apparent. In my humble opinion, the craft of illustrating is in the detail of the image being created, not in the knowledge of the animal's genetic origin, and that image of the little brown dog spoke volumes. I'd already told them via email they were rescues, so I wondered if they were perhaps confused with what 'rescues' actually are (?) Ok, it's fair to say that for the most part, 'rescues' are the crossbreeds, although the cages of UK dog shelters appear to be changing their demographic as more and more pedigrees are finding themselves homeless. Nevertheless, quite often there is some indication of the genetics based on physical appearance. Then there are the obvious breeds that end up in shelters, usually because of their breed, behaviour etc. Of course there are those who find themselves in rescue shelters due to an owner dying which is very sad, but whatever the reason, and in the UK there are many, the one outcome remains the same. Abandonment. This is true of UK rescues. However, when it comes to foreign rescues, their reasons for being homeless are reduced to just a few, the main reason being an overbreeding population of homeless dogs and a government that is not taking appropriate humane action in dealing with the problem. But let's not get judgmental and snobby about the luxury we find ourselves taking for granted as we busy about our daily life. It is fair to say that the wealth of a country is closely linked with its management of animal welfare and animal population control. With so much uncontrolled breeding and interbreeding, it's quite difficult to whittle a dog down to any number of breeds in particular, although for homing purposes, the charities who step in to find homes for these dogs have to put something down on paper, so they largely just guess. It's worth mentioning here that there are companies who offer DNA testing to determine the genetic make-up of your dog if this is an important factor to you. It isn't to me, and so I found it a contradiction in terms for anyone to ask 'what breed' is a street dog. And then it dawned on me. The confusion I had felt, the misunderstanding, which was as much on my part as on theirs, this '*need*' to know the dogs breed came from our own social conditioning. You see, they were looking at rescued dogs from a 'UK' perspective. I was looking at 'rescues' from a rescuers perspective. Talk to anyone whose homed a UK rescue and the first thing you'll ask (based on your observations) and they'll tell you is 'what breed is the dog'. Owners will summarize this information based on the initial feedback from the re-homing centre, and then picking this information apart, will turn to the physical appearance of the dog, colouring, and all the usual breed-specific embellishments before settling on a good explanation for 'their' final breed/s. They will positively glow when they are then invited to give the history of the dog. That is to say, the story that has been passed on by the previous owners or shelter re-homing the dog and reiterated a thousand times to anyone who will listen. The only one who really knows what's happened to the dog is the dog, and they're obviously limited when it comes to sharing that information. Feeling a concoction of pity and love, new owners will emphasise the devastating detail, leaving no horror out and arrive oozing with pride and gratitude to the moment when they got the dog home. They will continue for a while about the settling in period and end with 'the rest is history'. Their sense of achievement and pride is completely justified. Opening up your home to a rescued companion animal is a truly admirable thing to do. Forever-homing that animal is not only an admirable thing to do, it can be incredibly rewarding. However, forever-homing a foreign dog is quite a different experience as we touched on earlier in this chapter. For a start there are difficulties in identifying any specific breeds which many rely on to gauge temperament.

Speak to anyone who has been or is currently a 'street dog' rescuer and the first thing they will tell you, regardless of your genuine enquiry as to 'what breed is the dog?' is where the dog came from and of the situation the dog endured. They don't care about the breed. They care only that they have been proactive in removing this dog, this loving, lost and found soul, from a horrible situation. They will not always go into such detail about the dog's history because sometimes the detail is so harrowing. Who will it serve to continue to reiterate it? However, they will shine with pride and love when looking at their little 'fur-baby'. Silently swelling with pride at the internal knowledge of the challenges this sweet, stoic little soul has overcome. Yes, the journey over and settling-in-period may have been long and scary. And yes, it was tough, there may have been times of absolute desperation on the new owner's part and total confusion on the dog's part, but here they are, together, and loving life. The rest, as they say, *is* history. You see the most important thing to a rescuer of a non-UK dog is not the breed, it's the capacity to extend their compassion and their home to the most deserving and endearing souls without judgement, without the human conditioning of needing to label the dog, and with the only value being that which first and foremost is extended to the dog, resulting in peace of mind for the rescuer.

CHAPTER 2
THE BRAWN AND THE BRAINS:
LIFE ON THE STREETS.

The term 'street dog' is described in scientific literature as an 'urban free-ranging dog'. Needless to say the life of a street dog couldn't be further from the creature comforts of the domestic dog here in the United Kingdom. Even those UK dogs that have fallen on hard times would at some point have experienced some human interaction, especially as puppies. Everyone loves a puppy. I agree there are exceptions to the rule. There are always exceptions to the rule, like puppy mill dogs bred in solitary confinement, never given a break from the breeding cycle. But I'm not here to discuss the moral and ethical wrongs of UK dog issues. My purpose here is to make available some information about homing street dogs. Life on the streets can be tough and usually is, especially if there are many, as is the case in many countries worldwide, hundreds and thousands of dogs, all wanting the same resources, food, shelter and of course, the opportunity to put their genetic material into the future (as with all animals, wild or domesticated). Add to that the social conditioning of each country's people, many of whom see these dogs in the same context as many here in the UK see squirrels, pigeons or anatomically closer, foxes. Of course, there are many of us who happen to enjoy all animals, although I wouldn't want rats running around in clear sight as frequently as I see pigeons. So let's take a closer look at the survival techniques street dogs have to refine. For a street dog, the world is very different. There is no-one to take care of them or look out for them. They live on their wits and cannot afford to relax, despite their exterior projection. There's a lot going on in the mind of a street dog. For example, a raised voice for a street dog is usually followed by a kick. The force behind that kick can range from a shooing tap to the full force of a boot to any part of the dog's body, including the head. Sometimes the violence arrives before the voice, so they have to remain guarded at all times. A dog's natural behavior sees them living in dens, so they will dig holes in the ground to sleep or hide in at various times of the day and in various locations. After all, the more places a dog has to sleep, the less chance a dog has of finding itself involved in a challenge from another dog. The main enemies of street dogs are cars and unsurprisingly, the street dog catcher. They are sporadic in their arrival and come with nets, ropes, beating sticks and metal trucks with open rubbish chutes in which they dispose of the dogs in. Often bones are broken and brains are damaged when being thrown into these trucks. Dog catchers are as stealthy as the dogs; they have to be to make their job successful. Dogs collected by the dog catcher are not taken to a veterinarian where they are checked for disease and then put up for adoption. They are not taken to an adoption centre for the opportunity of being homed. Those that don't die in the trucks are most likely to end up in what is known as a 'kill shelter'. Kill shelters are buildings of absolute horror, where dogs are beaten with sticks, metal poles. They are also subjected to other unimaginable atrocities, many of which that too graphic to write about here, before they are finally put out of their misery.

This seems like an appropriate time to discuss animal sentience, so I'd like to start with the discussion on the validity of animal sentience as was addressed poignantly by English philosopher, Jeremy Bentham when he famously asked:

'The question is not 'can they reason?' nor, 'can they talk?' but rather, 'can they suffer?'

When asking this question he was referring to utilitarianism and addressing the topic of non-human animals as a whole, including those animals used in the meat and dairy industries. But let's take this valid statement and apply it to the topic in hand. Dogs are arguably one of the most intelligent animals on this beautiful planet. If you've ever had the pleasure of spending any time with a dog, you will have experienced that the conversation between the two of you was carried out predominantly in body language. Not only would it have been silent (unless it was with one of the more vocal types) but it would have been full to capacity and rich in emotion. There would have been a definite connection resulting in you both understanding each other perfectly. If man and dog can communicate so effectively, so efficiently despite the obvious barriers, imagine the depth of communication shared between dogs. And then consider the context of the communication between dogs in a kill shelter.

For those dogs that end up in the kill shelter whose howls and cries are audible to the human sense, it is harrowing. If you're an animal lover and a highly sensitive person like me, the slightest yelp from any dog penetrates my entire being, much like a mother and child, and triggers urgency in me to run to the dog and fix the problem. I want to always make things better for them. But for those dogs in the kill shelters, there is no escape. It does exactly as it is labelled; killing is the nature of the business. These dogs are pests, vermin in their own country. They are extended no compassion and shown no mercy. Death in these places is brutal. Dogs, like all animals tuned into their environment and their consciousness have a sixth sense. They pick up on vibrational energy and feel its impending arrival. For example, remember the tsunami in 2004 that struck Sri Lanka? How could anyone forget, it was one of the biggest human disasters in our history. In the days that followed this epic tragedy, it was noted that no animals were found near the area struck. Both wild and domesticated animals had felt it coming days before and moved to an area of safety. On a less dramatic note and a much smaller scale, my first rescued street dog continues to have psychological issues as a result of having been in a high kill shelter before being rescued, although much reduced from when she initially arrived. Doggy maintenance is a real issue for her. No matter how stealthy and relaxed I am at getting the nail clippers from the drawer, she knows before I've even entered the room with them and runs upstairs to hide under the bed. I've yet to clip even one nail after five wonderful years with her. When the dog catchers are in town with their nets, choke ropes and beating sticks, these dogs that are already acutely wired for survival go into overdrive. It really is do or die, and no animal wants to die.

Anyone with an ounce of compassion will admit to being mortified at the reports of cats and dogs having fireworks tied to their bodies and set off around November 5th here in the UK. For dogs living in some of these countries, they don't just have select holidays that celebrate with fireworks to contend with. This is a real danger every day of the year for them. The following information is not for the faint hearted or those of a sensitive disposition, but it is a further example of some of the violence street dogs are subjected to. While graphic in explanation, the following is mild in comparison to some of the brutality these dogs face. It is not uncommon for puppies and older dogs to be subjected to being spray painted, having their ears cut off, or their back legs hacked away at the knees. There are some very cruel individuals in the world who have yet to discover the joy a companion animal can provide. But until they extend and expand their compassion and understanding from the self to the world around them, they will continue to do unthinkable things to animals and often other people. I do not accept this unfathomable behaviour has any real excuse, but I am sure their social upbringing will provide ample explanations for their inexcusable and archaic behavior.

There are many reasons dogs end up on the streets. Many are born there and for them life is accepted as it is, tough and a do-or-die situation every minute of every day. But for some dogs, they weren't always on the streets. Some of these dogs had homes as puppies and for one reason or another, they are kicked out of their homes, abandoned on the streets or driven miles into the next town and dumped. They have little to no survival skills initially but they learn fast. They have to. I cannot even begin to imagine what this feels like to have a home one minute and then find yourself in completely alien surroundings, with no-one to feed you after you've been relying on them for however long, no one to make you feel safe and unsure of what and who is safe and what and who is not. Imagine waking and finding yourself in the middle of the most obscure land where you know no-one and are not welcome, it would be terrifying. Every single morsel of food that passes into the mouths of these dogs will have been begged or stolen unless offered up by one of the street angels who risk their lives to rescue them. Many food morsels would have been secured after having endured an altercation with another dog or being kicked or punched by a human. The food may have been poisoned or may cause other health complications. Veterinary treatment is limited for the lucky ones picked up by virtuous animal rights activists who often risk their lives to save these dogs, but for the majority of street dogs, it is non-existent. They will live on the streets with whatever illness or ailment they have until it heals, subsides or kills them. For bitches, life is the toughest of all. Not only will they have to navigate and match the survival skills of any other dog on the street, they will have to fend off the attention of unneutered dogs who instinctively want to pass their genetic material into the next generation. For many of these females, it is not uncommon to be literally hounded to death by the attention of males. Once pregnant, the demands on her body are tenfold. If she's lucky, she'll survive the pregnancy and have her litter of puppies. The puppies will then continue to put extra strain on her already malnourished and painfully weak body. If she is picked up by the dog catcher while pregnant, her condition will do her no favours. If she is taken in by one of the animal charities working to ease the street dog situation, she will likely have her puppies exterminated. I have to tell you here that spaying and neutering of dogs and cats in these countries leaves a lot to be desired. The medical practices are not as developed as they are in the United Kingdom, and not being a nation of 'animal lovers', they are fairly dispassionate about the whole procedure and aftercare. There have been many cases of rescued street dogs arriving in the UK after being spayed overseas and urgently needing veterinarian treatment to rectify the butchered mess that was left. Of course, life on the streets has its redeeming features for the dogs to some degree. They have the freedom to come and go as they please, do whatever they like and roam wherever they want. On the surface they appear pretty carefree, but it's a cost to benefit experience, often with life or death decisions. But for street dogs, as with all dogs, they live in the moment by their very nature.

CHAPTER 3
IT'S ALL ABOUT PERSPECTIVE:
PUBLIC OPINION

Whether you're pro street dog rescue or not is all a matter of perspective. I hope I will address this topic with enough foresight to cover all the obvious concerns, however with so many possible outlooks and personalities it would be impossible and foolish of me to try and account for all perspectives. So I will keep to the common reasons that street dogs and street dog rescue is criticised. Not really wanting to get political but finding no alternative, if we look at the recent surge in migrant rescue many wouldn't deny another human being the same human rights that they have, while others are unfathomably against the foreign influx despite the obvious and well-documented atrocities these people face. And while there is an undertow of racism in the UK, it would appear this intolerance is not restricted to humans. Discrimination of any kind is abhorrent and evil in its foundations, but regardless of opinion I think we would all agree discrimination is the result of ignorance and intolerance. For many who rescue and those who offer up their homes to street dogs, their values are much the same as they are for a fellow human. Their capacity to extend their compassion beyond man and encompass all living beings is truly magnificent and a true testament to what it is to be human. There is no discrimination against any dog, regardless of its origin, physical form or history. However, It would be unreasonable for us to not give some consideration to those who have no personal issue with any dog based on its place of origin, but whose disapproval of street dog rescuing is derived from taking into account the overpopulation of dogs in the UK. Many will make decisions based on what they know about the plight of animal welfare trusts. The Dogs Trust reported it rescued approximately 17,000 dogs across 21 centres in 2015. That's just one welfare organisation. As there are many more, both national and regional, we can correctly assume this number to be much higher. In 2016 the 'Stray Dog Survey' was released on behalf of the Dogs Trust. The purpose of the report was to investigate what happens to UK strays. While the stray dog situation in the UK is relatively out of sight in comparison to other European and Asian countries, the report gives some thought-provoking statistics. The data contained in the report was submitted by local authority dog wardens and environmental departments across England, Ireland, Scotland and Wales. Based on 352 authorities that responded to the survey, some 81,050 dogs were handled as strays between the 1st April 2015 and 31st March 2016. The report also looked at what happened to the strays. An estimated 54% were reunited with their owners, 9% were re-homed by the authorities and 22% were handed over to welfare organizations or kennels after a statutory period of time. The report states that these proportions remained about the same for the past 10 years. The estimated number of dogs put to sleep by the authorities who seized them from the street was 4%,that is approximately 3,199 dogs. It should be noted that out of all the authorities that contributed to the report, only half disclosed details of the destructions, that's just 55% of all cases, leaving 1,760 cases unanswered. 901 of those disclosed cases were due to aggressive behavior, which can largely be attributed to poor owner management and lack of training. 538 were destroyed due to ill health and 181 were destroyed under the Dangerous Dogs Act. Sadly, not all dogs destroyed under the Dangerous Dogs Act have behaved in a dangerous or aggressive manner. Sometimes it is simply a matter of being born the wrong breed. While this report documents the statistics to some degree, there are no reports to use as a comparison for non-UK countries that have a stray dog issue. But you can be sure the death toll is exponentially higher than here in the UK and is not even remotely humane. Until I did some research I was unaware of the extent of the dog population numbers here in the UK. However, these numbers are much lower in comparison to those of thirty years ago, thanks to the effective implementation of spaying and neutering. Regardless of the numbers, the fact that we have an issue at all is often all someone against street dog rescue needs to know. Knowing a little more about the statistics, it's easy to understand the reasoning, to some degree, of the bad feeling that some people feel the need to express. It doesn't excuse their behaviour as we all have a duty to exercise tolerance and respect others freedoms to make this a successful society. As someone who has experienced firsthand the disapproval from others when asked where my dogs came from, I feel it only fair to prepare you for what you might expect. The disapproval may come from some likely and some not-so-likely quarters. For example, I found that some of my extended family members were not so welcoming initially and one of my dogs was the recipient of outward disgust. Needless to say, my dog refuses to visit anymore...but seriously, I would just prefer not to subject him to that kind of negativity. He is a wonderful, loving and hugely funny boy and I won't let anyone crush his spirit. The veterinarian I used with my first two rescues appeared unbothered by my selection of dogs; in fact everyone in the practice welcomed them with treats and lots of fuss and attention. However, other street dog rescuers have reported feeling an air of disgust from their vets when acting responsibly and taking their new family member for check-ups. In this case, you may want to either just grow a thick skin and ride it out if it's a particularly good vet (although in my humble opinion a good vet would remain professional at all times, regardless of personal opinion), or if not, seek another vet to care for your dog. Dogs are hugely sentient beings that pick up on these moods and feelings.

You may even find that some dog walkers out with their dogs make comments if the word is out that your dog is not from the UK. They may even try to keep their dog away from yours. One of my neighbors wouldn't walk her dog when we were out and would give us a wide birth if she'd mistimed us returning from our walk. The fact of the matter is that some people will be convinced that your dog will be carrying all manner of pests and parasites and rather than getting the facts about the health care checks your dog would have gone through just to get here, they will just close off their minds and their hearts and dig in deep with disgust. You owe these people nothing, but should you ever find yourself with the opportunity to educate, please ensure you let them know of the three thorough vet checks your dog would have had before, during and after travelling. Also let them know that your dog would have been checked by a representative for DEFRA and would not have been released from quarantine if she/he was not fit to be in the UK. As you do this, fully enjoy the moment, that uncomfortable look you'll get when setting the record straight and opening a mind, then look at your dog, blow him/her a kiss and walk on with a smile on your face and love in your heart.

CHAPTER 4
MOVING ON UP: CHARITIES

Before we get into the nitty gritty of the work of street dog charities, let us consider the morals and ethics of what they do. On the surface and, with the exception of those who are ignorant to the work they carry out, most would agree that what they do is morally right. While it is often difficult to separate 'morals and ethics', they can be defined thus. Morals are born out of our sense of obligation. They are instilled in us from birth up and mould our sense of duty. Ethics are conceptual, arising from the inspiration of Plato and Aristotle. They are the work of the mind. The purpose of ethics is to act as a moral code. They are simply rules and regulations tied to our belief systems. Any thought that is true to you is a belief. The evolution of ethics has been relatively stable in comparison to how quickly things change in the modern world, but challenges from others in the field of psychology have seen three dominant schools of thought emerge. Deontology, related to acts carried out in line with one's duty, followed by consequentialism, which focuses on the outcome of the action. The final school of thought is virtue ethics, which essentially is ethics based around a person's character. For example, some might say those who rescue street dogs are virtuous; they are good by their very nature because they are caring. It is my understanding that the vast majority involved with street dog rescue practise virtue ethics. One might think that acting out our moral duty with virtue ethics is highly commendable and on the surface it is, as it's compatible with our very compassionate nature. However, while I agree in theory holding myself, I believe, the qualities of a virtuous person, I am not entirely convinced that this blurring of individual character ethics, in line with our sense of duty when working in charitable employment, regardless of whether it is paid or unpaid, is actually completely beneficial to all concerned. That's a little controversial and even perhaps hypocritical having rescued four street dogs, so allow me to explain my reasoning. Here in the UK we have a huge dog problem. There are hundreds, if not thousands, of dogs living in shelters as we discussed in the previous chapter. We have a huge underground dog fighting problem which occasionally finds itself the centre of attention when glimpses of it appear in the media. It's the main reason there has been an increase of incidents with dogs being snatched and stolen. Many of these dogs are used as bait dogs. We have a puppy mill problem where many dogs never see daylight and are kept in a perpetual cycle of pregnancy and birth. And we are a population of so called animal lovers, many of whom, with the best intentions, take on an animal and then neglect to care for it by failing to provide all of its psychological and physiological needs. The end result is that many of these dogs end up in shelters, being passed around different homes like sweets or are euthanised due to a lack of training, resulting in bad behaviour, frustration-aggression or fear-aggression. While the UK problem is predominantly out of sight (not on the streets), all but for the wonderful marketing of the Dogs Trust and Battersea Cats and Dog home, it is clear that more and more people are turning to the plight of non-UK street dogs. Google 'street dogs + (country of your choice)' and you will uncover some rather graphic documentaries of the sheer horrors and scale of the problem. It is not for the faint-hearted and is incredibly disturbing, so if you are of a nervous disposition, I don't encourage this. Social media has worked wonders to provide a platform for all of us, especially businesses and charities, but who are the people who run these charities? How easy is it for someone to acquire a dog? What checks are put in place to ensure that a person is suitable? What checks are made to ensure the dog is suitable? And what monitoring are they putting in place to ensure that these dogs remain happy, safe and in the right environment? I have some answers to these valid questions based on my own experience, but beyond experience, there is no literature that offers any guidance to the standards that these charities follow other than that which the charities produce themselves.

So let me start with my experience. My first rescue dog was not sought after. I mean I'd thought about getting a dog, but remember from the introduction, I had huge reservations. So I didn't go out on a mission to find her. I was merely sitting at my laptop, browsing Facebook and bombarding my friends with memes and 'pokes' (as you do). While scrolling through my newsfeed there was the most pathetic, scrawny little brown dog that looked like she'd all but given up on life. I immediately left a post on the wall where the image was being shared, asking, "Who is this dog and who do I speak to in order to rescue her?" My details were immediately passed to someone who sent me a private message. Within a week, I was booked in for a home check. The home check consisted of a volunteer from the charity coming to my home, checking out the security in the garden and house, asking me to complete a form, providing proof that my landlord was happy for her to be here and it was done. I was given no information on what to expect of my new street dog at all. I sent, what was, to me at the time, a large sum of money via Pay pal and Voilà! Within a month, this little brown dog was in my arms. She was absolutely terrified of people although she looked a lot healthier than she did in that first image I'd seen of her. I mean she had a little more weight on her. There were further issues which I'll discuss later in 'behaviour' but for now, the whole experience was straightforward, easy and extremely rewarding, if not a little disturbing initially. While I was waiting for her to travel over, I felt immensely guilty knowing there were many dogs here in the UK in shelters who would love a home. But I soon put that out of my mind by thinking about the horrendous condition this little brown dog was in, and who was on her way. I have to say, I don't regret one second of the effort I've invested for any of my dogs - those who live with me currently and those for whom it didn't work out. When the time comes (which is hopefully a very long way off) I would absolutely home another non-UK dog or dogs. I dare say there are many who have had a similar experience and, like me, have found that one street dog simply isn't enough! While many of those who work for charities across the board are, by nature, virtuous people, good, honest people, sometimes I wonder if logic gets lost over the sentimentality of 'doing the right thing'? Perhaps this is something that is evident in us all from time to time? I hold my hands up that, on reflection, this is something I am aware of in me. Perhaps this is a default setting for the human trait? However, when acting as a professional body for a highly emotive cause, one would like to think that restraint is encouraged and exercised out of necessity to ensure the least amount of error and upset.

My second rescue was already here in the UK. After a wonderful year of bonding, training and behaviour work with my first rescue, I felt it would be nice if she had some company. So I revisited the charity's page and enquired for a little dog to offer some enrichment to her life. I was told about a male dog that had been brought over to the UK but after just six weeks, he was no longer wanted due to the owner's health reasons. I checked out his pictures and agreed to meet him. Part of me already knew that, whatever I found, he would be coming home with me. And he did. He was what can only be described as 'detached'. This poor dog was so absolutely depressed. Within a day of having him, I noticed the most horrendous smell coming from his ears. I immediately took him to the vets. He had been here in the UK for six weeks and had been walking around with a severe untreated ear infection in both ears. I am unsure how this was missed as it smelt foul and his demeanor was extremely lethargic. I got him treated and returned to the vet several times with concern for a lump that was on his head. I was told it didn't look sinister and not to worry about it, but over the course of 18 months, it continued to weep and scab over. That was until one afternoon, whilst sitting on my sofa stroking him, the very corner of my nail just caught the scab which came off. I looked and saw a black but shiny lump just sitting there. Feeling a little squeamish, but curious to find out what this was, I gave the lump a little wiggle and 'ding', the lump fell out of his head and landed on my laminate floor. Grabbing a tissue, I picked it up and on closer inspection discovered that this poor boy had been walking around with a lump of lead pellet in his head. I was absolutely mortified! Someone at some stage of this dog's life had shot him in the head. This unfortunate dog had been through vet checks in his country that would have seen him fit for travel, although granted this wouldn't have prevented him from travel. Presumably he would have been taken to a vet on arrival in the UK, or at least seen by a vet when passing through DEFRA's procedure for incoming animals, so I was baffled as to how these issues had been missed. I contacted the charity to relay my concerns, both at the time of the ear infection discovery and, again later after discovering the lead shot pellet. There wasn't really much anyone could say about the ear infection.

I'm just relieved we got it treated as it must have been so painful for him. I was told by someone representing the charity that it was not uncommon for dogs to end up here full of shot. The information felt as though it had been delivered in a nonchalant way. No discussion was offered, or at least, the *very least*, the veterinary treatment that would be advisable for dogs entering the UK. I understand they are a charity and, as with all charities, resources are scarce, but I have to tell you, as someone who at the time was new to this foreign rescue process, I felt quite unsupported and concerned that there might have been other issues that either the vet or I had missed. I felt that I might not be providing sufficient care for this dog. I actually felt like I might have been out of my depth with the whole street dog rescuing thing. Wrongly or rightly, I always tend to assume that anyone acting on behalf of a cause, be it humanitarian or environmental, would be the expert on such issues. And if they're not the expert, they are at least prepared to research and put some planning or some kind of precautionary advice into action. At that point, I felt something was seriously missing from the whole process. Why wasn't I given any advice on what to expect once I had my street dog- medically, behaviourally, legally and socially? There are so many things that absolutely should be discussed prior to you signing a contract and handing over hundreds of pounds. And herein lies the root of the problem. Many of the people who work for street dog charities are volunteers. They have full time jobs, families, homes et cetera and are operating from virtue ethics - virtue ethics applied from their own characteristics which, individually are good and wholesome. They act from a place of good virtue and what it means for them to be involved in such work. If you've ever seen first-hand the horror these dogs go through in their own countries, you'll know it compels you to want to act. It's easy to see why their main purpose is getting as many dogs as possible out of these countries and into loving homes. However, there are costs and it does not always serve the dogs, as was evident initially with my second rescue. Scrutinising any charity is often met with disapproval. However, what you have to consider is that while they are registered as charities and gain social acceptance by default in obtaining charitable status for the work they do, they are often run like businesses, or at least they appear to be run like businesses. Mixing business with pleasure can be toxic, so if you are acting from a standpoint of virtue ethics, again, that is actions carried out based on characteristics and moral obligation from a personal perspective, you are quite likely to make choices based on your own judgements and not on evidence of the situation. When you have a whole troop of volunteers with various ideals, beliefs and reasoning for what is acceptable and what isn't, coupled with the inevitable lenience towards those known personally to the volunteer, the standards, safety and security of these dogs may get lost and end up in the wrong hands. The number one reason for ex-street dogs being re-homed is due to lack of information and misunderstandings. They are not like regular dogs, as we will discuss later. They are equipped for survival in what is, essentially, 'the wild', albeit a watered down wild as they live in urban areas. They have behaviour that is not understood and met with despair, making both the dog and the uneducated owner's life miserable in those early days. While maintaining this virtuous standpoint is very honorable in its foundations, street dog charities will assume to run like businesses, except they are usually quite disorganised due to their lack of time because of other commitments. With so many viewpoints involved in such an emotive undertaking, miscommunication and misunderstandings are inevitable, as was the case with my last two rescues. Having spotted a gorgeous little hound pup, again in my newsfeed, I proceeded to ask questions about her. Her story was sad, just as they all are. She had been pregnant and on Death's door. Male dogs were hounding her and she was horrendously emaciated. A visit to the vets saw her puppies exterminated and she was taken to a 'safe' area and nursed back to health. There was no question. I had to have her. In the same newsfeed, a few scrolls down was the sweetest bundle of white fluff with text saying she'd been thrown from a moving car. It was a done deal. Here were my two newbies! Because they lived so far apart, I felt it would be better for them to meet first to ensure they got on before travelling to the UK. The charity agreed this would be the best course of action. I had to personally send messages to arrange this myself, and due to demands in other areas of the volunteers' lives, response from anyone was slow and little, if at all. Making these arrangements should have been the work of the charity after all. Until the dogs were in my care, they were not my responsibility. By advertising these dogs, the charity is assuming responsibility. I put off signing the contracts whilst waiting to find out if the dogs would get on, and after weeks of waiting, was told that they were too far apart so wouldn't be able to meet before travelling to the UK (I suspect this was down to availability of both time and money for the charity). However, I was told another member of the charity would take one of the dogs off me if it didn't work out. I tentatively agreed, all the time thinking to myself that whatever happens, it will be fine, we'll get through it. I agree, this was indeed an equally foolish and selfish act on my part. It was a huge risk and one that didn't pay off, but based (stupidly or not) on the nature of my original two dogs and, on reflection, lack of education, I signed the contracts and emailed a copy back. At the time I was notified that I had been successful in my home check back in February, I was told that my new additions would likely travel towards the end of April, beginning of May. I was told that the charity had changed transporters since I last used them four years ago, so I accepted that perhaps this was the only available transport out. I left the conversation suggesting 'the sooner, the better'. Then in March I noticed that other dogs that had been advertised after my dogs were travelling to the UK. I was totally baffled and actually, a bit upset that I had not been told of this opportunity for them to travel. I made contact with the charity and was told that they were under the impression I had requested a late travel.

Needless to say, a long succession of emails was exchanged and the volunteer who was responsible for the misunderstanding nobly came forward. It had also come to light that one of my rescues was not going to be spayed before travelling, unlike my previous rescues. I had queried this and agreed that actually it was probably safer for her to have this procedure in the UK. There was a further misunderstanding about the 'donation' they required and what it covered, but this was quickly resolved when it was made clear to me that without the donation received in full, the rescues I had secured would not be travelling. I completely understand that the charity couldn't operate without money sent by individuals like you and me. However, I reiterate, if the information had been clearer from the outset, if the structure of the charity/company had been set up with set roles. That is to say individuals sticking to their own purpose within the charity. If there had been more structured rules and regulations carried out to inform prospective owners, there would not have followed such unnecessary bad feeling and confusion.

It is clear from this example that there is something to be gained from my experience for both those looking to adopt a foreign rescue and those working in foreign rescue charities. While anyone can set themselves up as a business or charity, there is a definite requirement for greater regulation within charities and certainly those charities that are essentially set up in the UK but whose operation is split between the UK and non-UK countries. Another feature you might assume within a street dog charity is that of a sponsor or a foster home. Often our emotional intelligence is overpowered by our desire to help ease the 'strain' on charities. We want to feel validated and worthy, and again, acting out of moral duty and virtue ethics. Many subconsciously seek social or personal acceptance in providing the financial assistance a charity needs, and then reflect on how terrible they feel by not receiving this unspoken validation request that was paid along with their cash. Despite your understanding of the word 'charity', and the assumed victim stance projected by charities (that's the nature of charity), the marketing efforts are incredible, and rightly so. Everyone does what they can to advance the efforts to ease the problem. But is the appeal to the UK public dealing with the root cause of the problem, or is it just plastering over the issue? For every dog taken off the streets, another will take its place. That's ecology for you. Only by working with governments of the country concerned while continuing to work to ease the issue with rescuing, can progress be made. A good example of this is the work of Animals Asia founder, Jill Robinson M.B.E. By negotiating and working closely with the Chinese government, Jill was successful in changing policy and overseeing the closure of bear bile farms across Asia. Off the back of this work, she went on to set up Doctor Dog and is tackling the cat and dog meat industry in Asia.

The role charitable volunteers acting under the organization adopt is basically from a good moral and ethical source. They are simply trying to save as many dogs as they can, but at any cost? To deny compassion and empathy to another human who is also acting from the same standpoint in the only capacity they perhaps can ,financially as a sponsor, is not (in my humble opinion) acting entirely out of good moral and ethical reasoning. The charity may feel they are making progress when 'pity donations' from their excellent marketing techniques come rolling in. But the fact they are now unable to provide the time and attention to thank those who have contributed to their cause and up-date them as to the status or situation of, in this case, a dog that has been sponsored, can eventually prove to only be futile as more and more sponsors make the decision to stop supporting them. Many of us will feel awkward, powerless and worthless when joining social media pages that keep us up-to-date with news when pleas for financial help are sent out about a dog who we desperately want to help, but are financially unable to. It feels like we've let them down in some way, especially when we then try to shut it out of our minds, but find ourselves wrestling with it for the rest of the day and possibly weeks that follow. This seems even more unfair when you've offered up your home to a dog and feel your conscience put under pressure to do more and more when you have no more to give. As awful as this feels initially, I advise that you absolutely not feel guilty. There are a lot of sad stories out there, and even if you had all the money to provide for all the dogs, you would not be saving all of them. The sheer scale of the problem is beyond the capacity of you, the individual, and, in fact, the charity. Of course, if many get involved in the charity, it may give the illusion of easing the situation, but to really impact the situation it will require a clear structure; organisation within the charity; a good relationship with the government of the country, and all parties working towards the same goal. Until the root cause is addressed by the government of the country concerned, humanely, as is the example of the UK by introducing rules for leads, spaying/neutering and responsible ownership, there will never be an easing to this situation. For every dog taken off the streets another female fills the space with 5-15 puppies. And so it continues generation after generation.

Foster homes are another option that street dog charities use. These are essentially half-way houses for dogs. Often, they are here in the UK, meaning that it's quite likely the funds you pay for your dog's travel will be spent on a 'foster dogs' travel if yours is not travelling at that time. Being non-government funded and relying solely on public donations, foreign dog rescue charities literally live a hand to mouth existence and while they are trying to do the right thing and fervently believe they are acting with the best intentions, there are always costs- if not financially, certainly emotionally, and always physically be it to them by sheer mental and emotional exhaustion, to those dogs who end up in the wrong situation, and the new owners who can very quickly feel overwhelmed, out of their depth and despairing. The one main concern I found when contacting the charity was that there was no telephone number to discuss any issues with anyone. Everything is done by social media, which in some respects is great as you have a paper trail of all the contact. It also works well if you have a good relationship with the charity or any of its volunteers. However, it also contributes to confusion and bad feeling when things don't go so well when words are read out of context, and meanings are lost on both sides. After such a mix of experiences with street dog rescue, if you are considering homing a rescue dog, I would strongly advise that you ensure the following before entering into any agreement with a street dog charity:

When asking about the dog you're interested in, get as much information as possible. Try to ignore any sentimentality that shows up. They will all have a sad story. This is a serious business for you and the dog, and a lifelong commitment. You are taking on a 'street dog' so you need to know as much as possible about it. Ask about any history this dog has. Health issues, behavior issues, spayed/neutered (when, where?), is it good with cats and children. Compile a list before the home-check arrives. Don't assume that because it's a street dog there is no history. The people on the ground picking these dogs up spend time around them and may know something that is vital to your decision in continuing with your intention to home or not.

While gaining information about behaviour around children and cats, take this only as an advisory. My last two rescues were not good with cats, despite being told they were. No information is given on how they test for this, under what circumstances or for how long. (I will explain more in behaviour about these two rescues). Aside from that, each animal is an individual and just as we don't get one with everyone, neither do animals.

During your home check, ask questions - Lots of questions. If the volunteer is vague about anything you ask, you need to go back to the charity online and get answers. If the volunteer is vague about how the charity works, be even more aware and definitely go back to the charity, enquire about the volunteer's credentials. This wasn't my experience, but I'm sure it happens. Any charity representative should know about the charity they are working for. If they don't it's a good indicator that this is not a well-organised system and you can expect problems.

If you're thinking of homing two dogs together and they live far apart, ensure they can meet before they travel and that, beyond words on a screen, this is absolutely possible and '*will*' happen. Ensure the charity will work to organise this. Resources or not, if they offer this or agree to your request for this, they should then carry it through, not leave it to chance. It is completely irresponsible for them to do so.

Before you sign any contract, find out the financial outlay and when it's due for payment.

Be absolutely clear about what you are paying, how it is to be paid, what it covers and get a receipt. If you are concerned about the legalities of the money, you can contact the appropriate authorities who will investigate your concerns.

Read the contract. The contract is not just a piece of paper that binds you to conditions, it also states the charity's role. Ensure they carry out their part. In my humble opinion, at least one further home check should be made to fully support the dog and new owner.

I hope this book will go some way into offering an insight into what it means to home a street dog, but if you have any questions at all about your dog, you need to ask the charity questions not only before they arrive, but throughout the settling in period.

Ask the charity about support systems that are in place for you as a new owner should it not work out or for when issues arise (and they will).

Not intending to put you off foreign rescue, it doesn't always work out. Unfortunately the internet amplifies the clique of groups on social media, especially those with an emotive cause which is being approached with a *family* feel, rather than from a business/charity stance. While you wouldn't expect such behaviour from an adult you should be prepared that you may well be faced with some pretty hostile situations when trying to get help. But stay strong and remain focused on who you are actually helping. You are not asking for anything but the safety and sanity of yourself, your family, your dog/s and other animals already residing with you. Stand firm and know you are doing the right thing by reaching out.

Street dogs are the most loving and wonderful companions but they come with baggage which you'll have to navigate whilst supporting your dog in its new and alien environment, before you take on any animal be sure you have all the information you think you might possibly need. This may not always be apparent to you. After all, you do not know what you do not know. But now you have some guidelines, I hope you will be better informed of the risks at least.

Get it in writing when your dog is travelling. Ensure you know up-front especially if you have to arrange care for other pets. Charities may be vague about when the dog is traveling due to the instability and use of unreliable transport in the country the dogs are traveling from, which is not helpful and, another indication of disorganisation. Keep asking. If they want to continue their work, they have to get organised or else risk losing potential homes.

I want to end this chapter by assuring you that the bulk of this chapter is based largely around my own experience and may not be a true representation of other charities. Furthermore, while I feel there have been significant flaws in the education of potential owners (which this book hopes to address) the work charities do for street dogs are highly commendable. The logistics, not only in getting the dogs here, but finding safe areas in their own country, the financial and legal hurdles they have to overcome is huge, and by no means a small undertaking. But despite their laudable efforts, as the potential owner of a street dog, you need to detach yourself to some degree from their plight and, think logically about the impact this will have on you and your family. Taking on a dog that has previous health complications will likely have assurances from the charity that assistance will be given with health care for the dog, but if the charity are operating on a hand-to-mouth basis, how can they possibly keep to this assurance?

If you're still reading and are unperturbed by the potential risks so far; have decided you want to rescue a street dog regardless of what that might mean, that is amazing! Having rescued two that are my world, I can tell you whole-heartedly, they are thoroughly rewarding.

You owe it to yourself and the dog to do your homework and choose well. More than that, don't be afraid to make the right choices for you and your immediate kith and kin and pets, regardless of public opinion.

CHAPTER 5
LEGAL BEAGLES: THE LAW

There are legal responsibilities that the charity will need to address in order for your dog to travel. And although these are legalities that the charity will take care of, you should be aware of them so that you can ensure your animal has legally entered and conforms to the law here in the United Kingdom. Since April 2016 it has been compulsory for all dogs living in the UK to not only be microchipped, but for the information to be kept up to date. Once you've collected your dog, if the charity hasn't registered them for you, you must contact Petlog to register the dog by giving the microchip number (which can be found in your dog's pet passport), a brief description of the dog, your name, address and telephone number. You can do this online and there is a small fee of about £15-£20 pounds. If you move house and the dog moves with you, you must update these details by giving your new address and telephone number (if it has changed). If you move house and the dog remains with another person at the previous address, the details will need to be updated if you were the registered keeper of the dog. There is a further administration fee of £5 each time you update the details. A microchip does not prove ownership of the dog. Rather it is a means of who is responsible for the dog should any other issues arise. Anyone not adhering to this law is liable for a fine of up to £500. Further information on the benefits and services provided to you by Petlog can be found by going to their website (listed in resources at the back of this book). Because you are registering a non-UK dog, you need to register under the 'foreign microchip' tab. The fact that they have a separate system for non-UK dogs just goes to show the sheer scale of the movement of street dog rescue.

*Costs/fees/fines correct at the time of writing.

Your dog would have been vaccinated against rabies, and a blood test would have been done about 30 days after the vaccination to ensure they are rabies-free and fit for travel. This blood test can only be carried out at an approved EU blood testing laboratory, so don't let anyone make you feel bad for taking in a street dog. They may have other issues, but chemistry-wise they are as fit as any other dog in the UK. The blood test will continue to be valid for as long as you keep your dog's rabies vaccinations up to date. If you are not planning on travelling with your dog, I see no reason why you should continue to put unnecessary vaccinations into your dog's system. It will not serve them physically or you financially. Your dog will also have been treated for tapeworm. The treatment will have been given no more than 120 hours (5 days) before entering the UK. We will discuss health shortly, but I would strongly advise that you re-treat your dog for all worms upon arrival as again, the treatment for worms is not always effective outside of the UK as I found out with my first rescue; although, that was over five years ago and medical treatment may well have improved by now. As a precaution I tend to re-treat all rescue dogs that come into my care. While some may view blanket treatment with some concern, I prefer to err on the side of caution, especially given the zoonotic potential and health implications for both the dog and humans. Details of the tapeworm treatment will be recorded in your dog's pet passport. Your dog will be travelling on a pet passport to which there are conditions that need to be met in order for your dog to arrive safely and legally into the United Kingdom. The charity you are sourcing your dog through is responsible for ensuring these checks are adhered to. When applying for your dog's pet passport, the charity would have had to produce the dog and all the medical certificates, along with the microchip number. It's highly likely that a veterinarian would have issued the passport. The passport will contain a description of the dog, any specific markings of the dog, details of vaccinations and worming treatments, and details of the veterinarian who approved them. When collecting your dog after it is released by DEFRA, ensure you receive the pet passport and any other documentation. If necessary make a checklist of the documentation you need to take with you and collect. It's very easy to get swept up in the moment of meeting your new baby for the first time.

This passport is your dog's document for life and contains the dog's medical history to some degree so it must be kept in a safe place. I tend to keep our dogs' passports with the rest of the family's so I know exactly where they are at all times. The passport is valid to travel on for approximately three years (or until the vaccinations expire) and contains vital information needed when taking your dog to the vet. Only a qualified vet can enter information into the pet passport. The passport will need to be presented with your dog for annual vaccinations. You will need to renew your dog's rabies vaccination if you plan on travelling with him or her at a later date. You should ask your vet about timescales for the rabies vaccination. These legalities have not been affected by the UK referendum and at the time of writing by the move to leave the European Union. If you are in any doubt, I advise you take the precaution of checking on the government's website for updates. Upon entering the UK, your dog will have to spend up to forty-eight hours in kennels while its health and documentation are verified by DEFRA.

As soon as your dog's health and legal checks have been successfully carried out, you will be able to collect your dog. All dog owners in the UK are bound under several laws. All are equally important which I intend to draw your attention to here, but I feel it is important to discuss with you the new amended Dangerous Dogs Act that came into effect May 2014. Regardless of the anomalies this act overlooks, the fact remains, it is the law and it applies to everyone who is in control of a dog. I strongly advise you to read the contents of this law and if there is anything you are unsure of, you should seek advice from a legal professional. Please don't be alarmed by this. I appreciate it sounds ominous, and believe me, when you read this law, you'll think that sounds ominous in places too, but you'll better understand my use of the word 'anomalies' as it clearly does not take into account the very nature of dogs. In fact, it almost denies them any right to behave naturally, which goes against the fourth of the five freedoms set out in animal welfare legislation since 1965, including that of the RSPCA, which clearly states, 'the opportunity to behave naturally'. Having said that, allow me to put this statement into perspective. There have been increasing incidents in recent years of family dogs killing children and attacking assistance dogs that are working. The cases that have been reported in the media have been UK-born family pets that had behavioural issues due to poor animal management on the owner's part. In light of this, I absolutely agree that this law should be in place for the protection of all. But there are parts of this law that are open to interpretation. For example, if your dog runs up to someone barking (the law does not stipulate if this is playful or aggressive) your dog can then be considered 'out of control'. It can be seized and destroyed. An overexcitable dog, however docile in character, can be considered 'out of control' and subject to the same outcome. Therefore, as the owner of a street dog, you, more than anyone need to take this law seriously and put in place measures to protect your dog from being misunderstood. Regardless of these (in part) overcautious rules and regulations, it is the law and anyone that owns a dog in the UK must know it and do everything they can to adhere to it to prevent unnecessary euthanising of an innocent animal. The size of your dog is irrelevant; this law applies to all dogs from Chihuahuas to Great Danes. Before we move on, I want to address the subject of dogs and children. While there is no specific law that I have found to deal with this topic, it should go without saying that you do not, under any circumstances, leave your newly acquired street dog alone with children, just as you would not leave any dog alone with a child. Young dogs and street dogs are more likely to nip/bite when playing as they have no concept of 'boundaries'. To assume the dog will gauge play and stop, or, that a child is capable of assessing the situation of play is irresponsible. Equally, you should not leave children to care for the dog and should discourage teasing of the animal by anyone. As an adult you are seen as liable under the eyes of the law if you knowingly leave a child with a dog, if the dog then bites or hurts a child, or anyone else.

The Animal Welfare Act 2006 applies to those living in England and Wales. Those living in Scotland and Ireland have their own similar variation of this law and should do their research to ensure they are informed. This law is set out to protect the rights of all animals to ensure they are kept in the right environment with the ability to behave naturally, that they are provided the correct care relating to their diets, exercise, prevention from pain, injury and disease, and that they are protected from human inflicted desirable breed-specific traits such as tail docking, which is now illegal. If you have never owned a dog previously, you should ensure you have made every effort to research the care needed. Furthermore, you should ensure, with honest and unclouded deliberation that you can provide every single protection for the dog, from the moment you meet, every single day and for the next twelve to fifteen years. A happy healthy dog makes for a good life for both of you.

The Clean Neighbourhoods and Environment Act 2005 demands that dog owners clean up after their dogs. Sadly, there is no poo fairy and just as you would find it disgusting to step out and into a steaming pile of dog doo doo's, others do not wish to share in your dogs digested meal either. Apart from the actual grossness of this, there are actual health risks to small children and other vulnerable people who may fall in the vicinity of excrement. Dog faeces have the potential to carry a parasite that can causes blindness along with other health concerns. The parasite concerned is round worm and the condition is called toxocariasis, otherwise known as 'Toxocara'. The parasite lives and lays its eggs in the digestive tract of dogs, cats and foxes. Infected animals expel the eggs when they defecate. While this infection is very rare here in the UK, this parasite has the potential to destroy vision when any contaminated matter (faeces or soil) enters into the mouth of a human. Using a bag designed for the disposal of your dog's waste is advisable, moreover actually disposing of it in a bin and not slinging it into another area of the outdoors once bagged is responsible and respectful of others who walk in the same area you do. If you are one of those people who think it makes no difference whether you leave your dog's poop on the ground or bag it and then dispose of it in a bush, consider the connection between faeces and flies. Faeces provide a perfect breeding ground for flies which in turn increases the spread of disease. Furthermore, wildlife and livestock may ingest the discarded excrement-loaded bag, which has the potential to cause serious health complications, putting a further strain on resources for wildlife charities and farmers.

In line with the Dangerous Dogs Act 2014, the Clean Neighborhoods and Environment Act 2005 states that no dog should be off lead and should not be permitted to roam onto others' land or property. Failure to follow this law could see you fined up to £1000.

The Anti-Social Behavior, Crime and Policing Act 2014 have been replaced by the Public Spaces Protection Orders as of October 2014. Dog Control Orders and Public Space orders do not affect Scotland but they do apply to England, Wales and Northern Ireland. There are designated areas where dogs are permitted and areas they are not. As a responsible owner you should ensure you have thoroughly checked out any area you are taking your dog if you intend letting it off lead, or if you intend using this area for regular walks. This advice comes from the dog's health perspective as much as it does the legal perspective.

The next law I want to draw your attention to applies predominantly to breeders. Please don't make the mistake of excusing yourself from it. If your dog is a bitch and you allow her to have even one litter of puppies, you are a breeder. I want to make clear here that the very fact you are considering homing a street dog is the result of an unmanaged dog breeding problem. Furthermore, I want you to take into account the number of dogs here in the UK requiring homes. It appears to me to be unthinkable and utterly irresponsible, and selfish for any rational person to breed their street dog. However, as street dogs are being allowed to travel unspayed/neutered I wanted to make clear your responsibilities if you decide to breed your dog, or if you allow your dog to come into contact with an unneutered male and the inevitable happens. The Breeding and

Sale of Dogs Welfare Act 1999 is applicable in England and Scotland. Wales has a similar law but with licensing criteria. Those living in Wales should seek this information out and ensure they are fully compliant with it. It is illegal to breed any dog under the age of twelve months. Some of these dogs coming over are still puppies themselves. As cute as they are and, as cute as you think their puppies would be, you have a duty of care to this dog, future dogs and society as a whole. After all, society isn't something separate from you. You are a part of it and your actions, however insignificant you believe them to be, have an impact. If you do decide to breed your dog, you must not produce more than six litters from the same dog and must not allow the same dog to have more than two litters in one twelve month period. You must not sell any puppy under the age of eight weeks old. Failure to allow the puppy to be fully nurtured and weaned by its mother can cause significant health and psychological imbalances to the pup and nursing mother.

The Control of Dogs Act 1992 stipulates that every dog out in a public place should wear a collar with a tag detailing the name and address of the owner. A telephone number is advisable but optional. This information can be written or engraved, however it would make more sense to have an engraved tag as the information is less likely to fade or be affected by environmental conditions. Some owners choose to leave a collar off their dog when at home, but as you are homing a street dog, you should be aware that escape is but a heartbeat away with some dogs, especially if they are new to you. I strongly advise keeping a collar with your details on your dog at all times. This eliminates any room for error or accident.

Community Protection Notices and Bylaws on Noisy Animals can see authorities issue an abatement order if your dog's barking is excessive and causes disruption to your neighbours. For anyone unsure of what an abatement order is, it is the authority's right to remove the offending article, be it a dog or a stereo. If you are served a notice and fail to address the issue, you could also be liable for fines and legal expenses. The Animals Act 1971 could see you liable for any damage your dog causes to public property. Third party insurance is advisable as a precaution and can be obtained from the Dogs Trust for £25. This is a one off annual payment that covers any number of dogs you own for up to one million pounds. It offers other added perks and protection and comes as a highly recommended investment, certainly given the changes to the Dangerous Dogs Act 2014. The Road Traffic Act 1988 states that no dog travelling in a vehicle should be a nuisance to or distract the driver at any time. Dog crates or seat belt dog clips are available to ensure your dog travels safely. If your dog is a barker, perhaps invest in a muzzle to prevent so much noise. While it may be cute for a dog to hang out of the window of a car and enjoy the air, and while it may be highly enjoyable for the dog, the results of an accident can be devastating. Keep your dog safe at all times. If you are out and about and involved in an accident where a dog other than yours is injured, you are required by law to give your details to the owner of the dog. If no one is in charge of the dog, it must be reported to the police within twenty four hours.

It is strongly advised you seek insurance for your dog, as you would with any dog. While the very word 'insurance' may cause you to recoil in horror whilst sucking in air, there are some very reasonable brokers out there. But do your research as some may not pay out as well as others when you need them most. There are plenty of options on the internet to research but I always tend to look on moneysavingexpert.com before going to any of the comparison sites, just to see what the general consensus is.

While there are enough laws to put you off ever wanting a dog of any kind for fear of accidentally doing the wrong thing, it has to be said owning a dog is highly rewarding for both you and the dog, and over 8.5 million people can't be wrong! As someone who is serious about providing the correct care for your street dog (as is evident by the very fact you're holding this book in your hand) I see no reason why you would not want to be aware of the law in order to protect your dog for its entire life. You are one of those wonderful, responsible owners and I commend you for your efforts. Should you continue with your decision to home a street dog, I know you will both share a long, safe, and happy life together. That's all anybody could hope for, regardless of from where the dog originated.

CHAPTER 6
VET CHECKS: COSTS AND BENEFITS

As I've already touched on the vet checks that your dog would have undergone prior, during and after travelling, I'll omit them from this chapter, but by all means refer back to them in the 'legal' section of this book if you are unsure of anything. I wanted to reserve this chapter for the vet checks and possible health complications that you may have to work through once you have your dog. It is fair to say, not all vets look on street dog rescue favourably and while they may not approve of your new companion, in my humble opinion, no vet worth their salt would turn away any animal requiring treatment. If you're as lucky as I am, you will find a wonderful vet who embraces and values all life, regardless of his stance on UK dog populations, and positively welcomes responsible pet ownership regardless of the circumstances. With veterinary care and medication being more advanced in the UK, it is highly recommended that you book your dog in for a full and complete check-up within the first week of its arrival. Many surgeries offer a healthcare plan that helps spread the cost of vaccinations, flea and worming treatment with two 'free' vet checks per year, a good thing if money is a bit of an issue. Plus there are other added benefits that offer money off spaying and neutering as well as introductory offers on food and dental hygiene if you take out one of these plans. They are very good value for money and are highly beneficial to your dog. As with all dogs, the dental care of your dog affects the overall health of your dog. Investing in a dog toothbrush and toothpaste might well be a good investment with dental hygiene being fundamental to good health (and the most expensive to repair) but actually brushing the teeth daily may prove a little tougher. Building up a daily routine as you have for your own bathroom routine might seem like a bonkers suggestion but will benefit your dog. Street dogs are seen very much as vermin in their own country (and by some in the UK), they are often violently abused, butchered and wholly uncared for. As such it is highly likely that your dog may have been shot with an air rifle or pellet gun (as I discovered with my second). The location of the pellet/s may be many or may be one, and may go undetected for months or even years. Lead is a toxin and can cause blood poisoning. Some symptoms can include vomiting, diarrhoea, lethargy, poor appetite, abdominal pain, weakness, uncoordinated movement, hysteria or extreme anxiety to name but a few. My second rescue showed only lethargy and clumsiness. His depth of perception and spacial awareness was quite impaired at times. If you spot any of these signs alone or with any suspicious lumps report them to your vet and insist your vet carries out a biopsy. Don't leave it to chance even if you are told it looks like 'something and nothing'. It would be beneficial for your dog to have a full and thorough health check upon arrival. There may also be issues with weight as many of these dogs are malnourished and some extremely emaciated when picked up off the streets. Some can barely stand and those that can stand may have joint or organ issues. If you take on a street dog that has experienced or is currently experiencing some weight issues you should have this monitored closely by your vet and act on any dietary advice given by a qualified vet only. I mentioned earlier that many spayed and neutered dogs are finding themselves needing urgent medical attention once in the UK for a sterilisation operation that has gone horribly wrong. While in the UK this is a fairly straightforward operation, although not without possible complications, abroad it is carried out in the crudest of applications. A UK animal (female) being spayed can expect to have keyhole surgery whereby a small incision is made in the abdomen and the ovaries and uterus are removed. After surgery she can expect a following check-up to ensure all is well and healing as it should. The procedure in other parts of Europe may consist of a rather large wound resembling Frankenstein science where only the fallopian tubes are cut or tied. They will then be stitched up with whatever material is available, low grade medical suture if they're lucky, and receive no after care. Secondary infection is highly likely and the risk of death increased. Sterilisation complications are not isolated to females, although they are indeed more common. Regardless of the gender of your dog, a thorough examination should be sought to ensure optimum care and precautions are being taken. While it is in the dogs best interests to have the operation done here in the UK, this is another added cost that you will need to consider. As street dogs are exposed to all manner of parasites and diseases, it would be completely naïve of you to assume that your dog is parasite-free. As we've already established, your dog would have undergone checks to arrive here and be chemically and physically fit, but there is always the possibility that other parasites may go undetected, ticks are quite common and pose mild threat, while others may not be so obvious. For this reason, you should always seek a thorough health check as soon as your dog arrives. The range of possible pests, pathogens and parasites is huge and before 'anti-street dog rescue' people start getting all sure of themselves, they are not restricted to the street dogs, although by the very nature of street dogs, they are, of course, more exposed to them. However, as street dogs, their immune systems may become better equipped to fight off any number of potential illnesses. Until such research is carried out, it is unclear what the true implications are. But whatever the consequences, it doesn't make the dog any less worthy of rescue or treatment. It simply means that the dog requires more intensive care from a qualified veterinarian. And finally, it goes without saying that street dogs get into fights for resources as much as they are victims of human abuse. Naturally, wounds and broken bones healed and unhealed are also a possibility. If you notice anything and are concerned, don't hesitate to mention it to your vet. Even if they dismiss your concerns, it's better to have them dismissed than allow the dog to possibly suffer by not mentioning it. After all, it may be nothing, but equally it may be something and, as you are presumably not a qualified vet, you should not be diagnosing your dog.

Occasionally, things really don't end well and you may find that having invested your money time and effort, you have no alternative but to have the dog euthanised. 'But it would have had vet checks and been declared fit for travel' you say. Well, yes, but sometimes there are underlying problems that are missed and become exacerbated by the sheer physical stress put on the body during the huge journey over. Sometimes issues that had been missed may come to light and with no prospect of improvement, leaving the owners to have to make the difficult decision to have them put to sleep. This is a devastating decision for any pet owner, and certainly the fact you've invested so much more into this animal makes it that much harder. Please know that if it comes to this, you did everything you could and you acted in the best interests of the dog. Be kind to yourself and your dog, remember them and celebrate the life they had and the fact you blessed each other's lives, however brief.

CHAPTER 7
NOT IN THE DOG HOUSE: BEHAVIOUR

And so we come to the chapter that will most likely deter you from your choice in offering up your home to a street dog. Unless you are 100% committed to the cause of street dogs and their plight or are smitten in love with one you've seen, this is the chapter that will absolutely drive the nail in the coffin of your decision to not home a street dog. But I feel it is important that potential owners of street dogs are made aware of this issue that many street dogs arrive with, especially in those early days. It goes without saying that this information is missing from the entire process of street dog rescuing over the internet. You see for many of those who have street dogs already, had they have known this information in the beginning, they perhaps would not have continued with their decision to home a street dog. But of course once the dog is there, what can you do?! It feels instinctively cruel to abandon a dog that has travelled by truck for many days on land, gone through numerous checks, just to be left in a UK kennel because of a toileting problem, amongst others. And it is inexcusably irresponsible to add to the UK dog problem in this way. So clue yourself up before the big day, expect the worst and you may be pleasantly surprised. The practicalities of owning a street dog mean a big adjustment for you and your family in those very early days and because the topics are so vast, I have sectioned them up. This list and the points raised are not exhaustive. There could well be other issues that I may not be aware of, but I have addressed the ones that I have experience in, or have heard of from forums. So settle down with a cushion (while you can) and prepare for the ride.

Diet

Your street dog will have spent its life raiding bins, fighting for food and scrounging for scraps. Suffice to say, its digestive system is not used to the benefits of high quality dog food, nor is it prepared for large regular meals. It is quite common for street dogs to suffer with digestive issues, so little and often is usually recommended and, preferably something quite bland. This is true even for UK dogs having a change of diet. You will hear all sorts of opinions on the right diet, but only you can really decide what you want to feed your dog. Of course human foods are not encouraged as they are full of sugar and salt, and are usually high in fat which a dog's body just doesn't cope well with and usually results in organ damage and disease, obesity or all three. I know they were street dogs once, but they wouldn't have been eating the luxurious foods that you and I eat. It would literally have been scraps, few and far between at that!

Foods that you absolutely must not feed to your dog include:

- Chocolate or any chocolate based products
- Onions, Garlic, Leeks or Chives
- Grapes, Sultanas, Raisins or Currants.
- Food that contains an ingredient called xylitol (typically in some peanut butter)
- Ethanol (found in alcoholic beverages).

All of these foods are highly toxic, so while I don't encourage it, if you are one of those 'cupboard love' types, please be extra vigilant on your food labels before feeding tidbits.

When considering your preferred choice of food, try to opt for one that has low sugar content. Some of the well-known brands, although gloriously celebrated and beautifully advertised, are surprisingly high in both fat and sugar, which is not good for your dog's health. Some people feel a raw diet is the best option and prepacked raw meats are available from various pet shops. However, always check the date and place of origin, and ensure you store them correctly away from your own food. Ideally you're looking for UK origin with a good time frame of at least one month before they are out of date. You should also consider the age of your dog when choosing a diet, as high protein diets can be detrimental to older dogs as they put added strain on the kidneys to process. Some might even look to the anatomical design of the dog and consider that it is not a strict carnivore and therefore should be eating a diet of meat and vegetables. Whatever you decide, do it slowly and be prepared to clean up any digestive disturbances. Dog treats, or as we like to call them in our house, sweeties, (they come running every time!) should be avoided initially. You can introduce them gradually but, to begin with, stick to just their main meals little and often, until they build up a stronger constitution. However, when you do introduce treats, I don't advise you give them all the time. They are not really any good for the teeth as they, too, can be loaded with sugar. Again, this is down to a matter of choice, but pay attention to your dog's behaviour and health when introducing new treats. Developing bad behaviour could well be the result of too much sugar. It is not advised you feed your dog uncooked bones as they can splinter and cause injury to the mouth. Having two dogs, we tend to avoid bones to prevent arguments erupting as well. Another very important but, perhaps, not so obvious issue is the dog bowl. At no time in a street dog's life would it have come into contact with eating from a dog bowl. Naturally, your street dog may at first refuse to eat from a bowl, as we discovered with our first rescue. We literally had to transfer all her food from her new shiny bowl to a small shallow plastic cat bowl, and even then she was hesitant about the whole process. Food is very much psychological and your dog may be pretty freaked out by these new rituals, so take it nice and slowly and give your dog time and space to adjust. Leaving the food down is an option if you have no other animals around, but I wouldn't recommend it in the early days. Remember, your dog may have a history of fighting for food and may well see the family cat as competition! There is every possibility that your dog will be rather protective over its food. I try to discourage this by not making food an issue. Whenever my dogs are eating, I purposefully walk past them and gently pat their rumps, give them a little stroke while telling them that they are good dogs. Once they realise there is no more need for competition and you're not going to remove the food source, life becomes a whole lot calmer. I do stress that you err on the side of caution when doing this and correct any bad behaviour with positive reinforcement. Each dog is different and although this is the nature of my dogs, it may not be the nature of yours. An example of positive reinforcement I used was to put a little food down at a time. Just as they're finishing, I pick the bowl up and fuss them at the same time. I wait for about fifteen minutes and then put a little more down, fussing and stroking them all the time. We associate food as being a good thing instead of a resource that has to be guarded. I also feed one of my dogs (my first rescue) in a separate room as she refuses to eat otherwise. Occasionally I trick her and put food or a treat down near the other so that she remains fully integrated, and doesn't isolate herself. This also desensitises her about eating with others which may evolve into territorial displays, if not addressed, and lead to a sick and depressed dog. Water should be made available at all times. I keep the water bowl fresh and topped up as the same fussy eater is a reluctant drinker and doesn't like dipping her head down into the bowl but will happily take from the surface. And finally, your dog may have a tendency to chew everything and anything. This may be out of boredom (if indoors is not as interesting as outdoors), frustration (anxiety about being kept indoors after always having lived outdoors), or over stimulation (there are just somany exciting and interesting textures and smells. All must be investigated and thoroughly tested). Teddies seemed to be a firm favourite in our house but were not exclusive. There were many tears initially when much loved and irreplaceable soft toys were found limp, eyeless, nose-less and with a fair amount of stuffing outside of the body.

My advice, if you value it, ensure you pup-proof it even though you are essentially dealing with an adult. Don't underestimate the ingenuity and tenacity of your dog!

Training your street dog to not chew is possible but you should absolutely expect that in those early days, everything is game. More importantly, if you suspect your dog has swallowed anything that could cause an obstruction be it wool, leather (book marks we discovered, thankfully expelled out on a walk), or even a whole teddy bear, you must contact your vet and have the dog thoroughly examined.

Urinating

If you're still reading, congrats! You really are serious about this and I'm glad you've taken on the responsibility to research thoroughly and make your decision wisely. If the last section didn't put you off, this one might. But read on and good luck.

This is the one issue that pretty much all street dog rescuers have to contend with and find utterly despairing. This is the one issue that drives a huge wedge of disappointment between you and your new best friend and it's heart-breaking that more isn't done to forewarn potential owners of this issue. For some reason, despite knowing you're rescuing a street dog, the topic of urinating and defecating is assumed to be much like that for a dog here in the UK. And for a puppy in the UK this is expected. By the time a UK dog reaches adulthood, and certainly if it's coming from a rescue centre it will be house trained. But for a street dog, an adult street dog at that, bizarrely, this is also expected. We just assume that they will know where the garden is and use it, or know that walk time is coming and save it up especially. We assume the charity will have put some house training in when housing these animals in safe areas. I fell prey to the same stupid thinking and guess what? Wrong! As a new owner of a street dog, you better be on this and prepared to kiss goodbye to your plush carpets or expensive flooring, for in the wild, when a dog has to go, a dog has to go. And if it's coming from an adult dog you could be staring at the mother of all messes. Or you may find, like your feeding patterns, they are little and often. The sheer number of exasperated posts I've seen about this very topic have left me shaking my head in disbelief that potential owners' are not being forewarned, which in turn leaves me feeling sad for the dog that is quite likely receiving some degree of anger and frustration from the owner, and is just feeling so confused by the whole situation. I'm not suggesting that charities mislead people, but I am suggesting that they don't give the necessary information to people who are essentially ignorant of what it means to house a street dog. I was blissfully unaware until my first arrived and then it was too late. Truth be told, even if I'd known, it wouldn't have put me off. I would have just prepared anyway, but it would have been nice to have had some warning. And guess what, it gets better! Just when you think you've nailed toileting, the slightest upset and '*boom*', indoors becomes the outdoors all over again, as we again discovered when getting our neighbour to house-sit and dog-sit while we went away for our first holiday in years! Now we just take them with us and do UK dog-friendly holidays. There are some very good deals to be had in some wonderful locations. Another consideration is male dogs will cock their legs, not even just to pee. The urge to scent is instinctive and until they settle, they may well shower your sofa or any other item of furniture just to make sure everyone knows 'this dog's in town'. In order to train my dogs, I used puppy pads which are literally training pads for the floor to soak up urine. I just edged them closer to the back door, along with regular garden visits, more frequent to start with, and gradually reducing to every hour, two hours and three hours, with positive reinforcement of praise and veg treats (food orientated dogs will do anything you ask of them) until, we finally had well trained pups. This was truly a day to behold and, boy, did we celebrate. It is hard work and extremely tiring, you have to be determined. I was fortunate enough to be home all day so could remain consistent with the routine, but if you have to work, you might want to consider your options and plan carefully. Perhaps puppy day care might be something you would consider? It's not easy by any means and the smell can be horrendous, but you must persevere if it is to improve. Another more serious issue is that your dog may well take to urinating on your bed. Your dog is not doing this to test boundaries and push your buttons. It is doing this as a mark of respect for you. It is saying, 'I totally respect you and you have full control'. It may also be the result of spaying/

neutering if the dog is sleeping on the bed. It's quite common during recovery of these operations, which can take some time to settle down, especially in bitches that have been spayed too early. If you are worried about this, or concerned for any reason, prevention is best, so put in place physical boundaries so your dog can't get into the bedroom. Shut the door and ensure everyone else in the house keeps it shut too. It will calm down and eventually stop, but it is no fun going through this. It is not recommended that you shout or smack your dog or use any heavy-handed techniques when dealing with toileting issues. Your dog will not understand this and may attack out of fear. Your dog does not speak English or any other language requiring intricate human linguistic abilities; it speaks dog which is mostly body language with sound cues, so you should address your dog with positive actions and assurance to get the best out of him or her. It's also worth mentioning that some cleaners contain ammonia which actually encourage soiling. Your best option for a cleaning product is one containing a bacteria-digesting enzyme. This eliminates not only the smell but any bacteria that may form from repeated soiling in the same spot.

Walking

Walking on a lead is as unnatural as it gets for a dog and is something your street dog may never have encountered before. However, if it's been lucky enough to have been housed in a pension (a safe area) it may have had the opportunity but you will have no idea if this is the case, so better to assume it has no previous experience. If you think walking a wee pup is tough, try walking an adult on lead for the first time. This is a new and strange concept to street dogs and may take some time to settle down. One of our rescues was so strong, I physically couldn't hold her, added to which, I discovered she liked cats a little too much when walking her for the first time. It was frightening. I was terrified she would get away and get hit by a car or find herself lost, or worse, waiting to be euthanised for being considered 'out of control' which she essentially was.

I highly recommend if this is your first dog, you seek dog training classes or else you may well end up completely regretting the whole idea of getting a dog via this route. It is hard work. They have no concept of obedience as they've never connected with anyone before. In the past, a walk anywhere has always been of their choice and if they chose to weave in and out of bushes, cars, houses (take your pick) they will surely weave. If your dog is anything like my second, despite puppy classes, he is what can only be referred to as a 'stop'n'start' kinda guy. At first it was exasperating walking ten paces and then stopping while he reads the news and scents the area, then another 10 paces and repeat. It took us hours to get around one walk route. But over time, he's learnt that a walk means we actually walk rather than amble. Although an amble is nice sometimes and, truth be told, I quite like that he has retained his character, it's all part of his charm. If, like me walking involves more than one dog, I will warn you now, they have no concept of sticking to a set path on the path. They will weave and tangle the leads up unless you take control. There are various approaches to walking your street dog and whichever one you take, be mindful that off-lead is not really a good idea to begin with. Many people (me included) opt for training leads. The size is easily adjusted and they are ideal for taking your dog to a large field where they can run around without you worrying about them disappearing through the fence. However, training leads are not good if you have a strong dog that pulls. Once you've let out the lead to its full extent, you'll then be wrestling like a tug-o-war to get that dog back to you.

If your dog is particularly friendly, as one of mine is, a short lead is advisable (remember the Dangerous Dogs Act 2014). I would hate for his friendliness to be misconstrued as anything other than friendliness. A shorter lead keeps him closer to me, leaving less room for misinterpretation. Recall is not always something you can train a street dog in. Mine have zero recall skills, so off-lead is not an option. One of mine is a nose-to-the-ground type. One whiff of a good or interesting scent and, he's focused and oblivious to any of my calls to return and, in fact, to anything else going on around him. Another option you might like to consider is a harness, but I don't recommend this in those very early days. We purchased ours after a year or two, once we knew our dogs well. If you decide to opt for a harness, ensure you measure your dog well and order the right size. I found the harnesses gave our dogs a feeling of more freedom, despite not being able to run off-lead, without them actually being out of my control.

In the first few days of walking with your dog, you are advised to double lead your dog, literally a collar and lead and another lead that slips over the head. Street dogs can be highly skittish and can easily slip their collars. They are wily. They've had to be to survive back home. Until your dog builds up trust in you and its new environment, you must use positive reinforcement and kindness to build that trust while keeping your dog safe and under control at all times. Another thing your dog will not have encountered is stairs. Stairs are a complete novelty and watching your dog trying to navigate them in those early days is both entertaining and worrying. My family and I ended up putting a baby gate up to stop them falling down the stairs once they'd successfully got up and to prevent them getting upstairs once down. It took a good couple of weeks before they had a good grasp of them. For your street dog, there are many new and unfamiliar sights and sounds outside here in the UK, many of which your dog would not have experienced before. Your dog will be in survival overdrive in those first few days and weeks as it tries to work out threats and non-threats, which ultimately means your dog may be quite fine one minute and skittish the next. Keep a good hold of the lead or leads and ensure your hand is through the handle and over your wrist with your hand holding on to the top of the lead length. Any sudden movements will be better secured against sudden bolting. As with any training, it takes time to build up trust and a good routine, but it will all come good in the end.

Playing

Our first experience of street dog rescue came with a rather bitter sweet realisation. Our little dog had no concept of play at all. We had assumed she would know about play and invested in lots of toys for her. But when she arrived we threw the ball and she just looked at it. No amount of exciting instigation would rouse her. She actually had no concept of play whatsoever. Some dogs may just take to play and know what to do, like I said in a previous chapter. Some of these dogs would have had families at some point before being kicked out, but there are many who really have started life on the streets with nothing and no-one. However, in order to keep your dog mentally stimulated you should provide a wide variety of toys to chew, hide and bury, and routinely encourage play. Trust me, it will come and when it does it brings unexpected tears of joy. Another unexpected joy we discovered is that street dogs are prone to digging. You may find food, toys or other household items chewed and buried in your bed, under cushions, under your sorted pile of laundry and anywhere else that offers the security of cover. Furthermore, if you treasure your lawn, be on guard when your dog is out there. I've experienced what can only be described as large craters in my garden that literally took minutes to dig. Back home, digging at speed may have been the difference between securing a spot for the night and being subjected to walking the streets in the cold and wet. It may also mean keeping cool on hot days. Our first rescue enjoys nothing more than digging a good hole on beach days and laying in it to keep cool. She'll also 'dig' under cushions on the sofa to hide on those days when she's feeling a bit 'off'. Street dogs are quick and efficient diggers and you should be aware of this.

Some dogs will have no trouble in playing but will be unsure when they have overstepped the mark. Rough and tumble can be every dog (and man) for himself. Positively reinforce gentle play by using consistent happy tones. Some people will use negative punishment such as removing a toy when play gets too rough. This teaches the dog that actions have consequences, but I would encourage that you opt for positive reinforcement over negative punishment. You can learn more about behaviour and training in my forth coming book. Do not shout, berate or beat your dog, just let your dog know in a calm and controlled way where the line is. Eventually he/she will realise and play will become a nice balanced event for you to both enjoy. Toy retrieval may be something that you can work on with your dog. My dogs took a while to grasp the concept and really enjoy this now - At least they do in the house. Outside of the house it's only one of my dogs that likes to play and once he's located his stick of choice, you've got two hopes of getting that stick off him…and one's Bob Hope (the others no hope, in case you were wondering).

Training

The main issues, spoken or otherwise, that concern potential owners of street dogs or neighbours who are aware of a street dog moving into their area is that of possible 'dog bites'. In all my time of street dog rescue and, in all the forums I've seen, I have only read one post where an owner expressed a concern about the dog guarding a child and not letting adults near it. While this is clearly a cause for concern, I can't comment on what led that dog to behave in such a way. I have no information on the way that family was with the dog, how long they had the dog or what led to those circumstances. Personally, and fortunately, I've never experienced anything like that with mine. That's not to say it will never happen, simply that in five glorious years of my experience of street dog rescue, I have never come across this. In my experience, street dogs are better behaved in terms of social acceptance than any UK dog I have met. I've been bitten by three dogs in my life. All were small breeds, all UK born and all pedigree, a Jack Russell, a Chihuahua and a Border Collie. While some may feel intimidated by the term '*street dog*' the fear is usually built up in their mind, born out of ignorance and perpetuated by common public misconception. Many serious dog bites are the result of fear and/or frustration, occasionally there may be an under lying neurological condition, but for the most part it is poor ownership that causes this result. Even with other dogs, street dogs have the highest grade of socialisation skills and are a joy around other dogs. Again, having said that, there are exceptions to the rule and altercations are more likely in smaller spaces, like your house, as it can feel quite claustrophobic in comparison to the abundance of space back home and outside. We had to let our last two rescues go due to the four way fights breaking out between the dogs. It was an incredibly difficult time for everyone. Our original two rescues, who adore each other, first felt a little unsettled, this I expected. However, what I didn't expect was my first rescue to literally make herself as invisible as possible for the first few days, until she reached a point where she could take no more. She lunged at the bigger of the two newbies who then lunged back, triggering the second newbie to join in, followed by the second original to defend 'his friend'.

It was just chaos. Had another family member who is bigger, stronger and quicker than me not been around, I have no idea how I would have stopped them. On top of that, both new dogs were aggressive towards one of our cats who, not only belongs to my young child but who, ordinarily lays and plays with our original rescues. The poor cat was so frightened and confused as to what had happened to her home, and I was scared that my young daughter might end up in the middle of the two newbies trying to get the cat. Eventually, we made the difficult decision to let them go. We contacted the charity and arranged for them to go into foster care. Within a matter of days, one of them had been snapped up by someone else. The second took a little longer to find a home but is now also in a secure home. It wasn't easy letting them go having invested so much in them, having waited so long for them and, having spent so long loving them in our hearts, but it was the right decision for everyone involved. Within forty-eight hours of them going, the house had settled down. The little dog was not completely back to herself but certainly better and the cat was still alive! For the humans of the house however, the tears and heartbreak lasted much longer.

In nature it always tends to be the small animals that are the most unpredictable and do the most damage, but never get complacent and assume your dog won't bite (as demonstrated above with the little timid dog), all dogs possess the means to bite if provoked. Regardless of how docile I know my dogs to be, I remain vigilant of their body language when around other dogs and children. If the tail's wagging then it's looking pretty good, but again, it can take but a moment for the situation to change and a wagging tail doesn't always mean 'happy', so remain observant. All dogs require training with no exceptions, and some dogs require a firmer handling, but that does not mean brute force. It simply means firmer in instruction and consistency. The trick is to get the dog to connect to you and your voice. You want absolute respect from the dog and for the dog, absolute love and connection. Once you have that, you can do pretty much most training, although, distraction is a big thing with street dogs, so don't expect things to move fast. And even if they do appear to be moving along nicely, there are relapses that may leave you baffled as to what changed. Stick with it and remain cool, calm and connected with your dog. Trust is crucial at this point. The level of training is really down to the owner. I'm not one of those people who likes to have complete dominion over another animal, therefore some of the more egotistical behavior that some enforce on their dog is not something I enforce on mine. I want to enjoy my dogs' and, in that, I embrace their characters, including the cheeky bits. I believe training should cover the main safety points like sit, stay, come, down, drop it and leave it, enough to keep the dog safe and retain some of its own character. Excessively trained dogs, in my humble opinion (with the exception of working dogs) are not allowing their true colours to shine. In the same way that a heavily criticised child withdraws and tentatively tiptoes around adults as if walking on eggshells, so too does the over trained dog. Being ever eager to please but, terrified and constantly anxious about doing the wrong thing. That's no life for any dog. The approaches and methods to dog training are many, and although dog training is largely unregulated, the science behind the methods known enable us to understand our canine companions and our training results better. However, the topic is so large I have opted to save this for a forthcoming book.

Training crates are a great idea as street dogs tend not to understand a 'naughty step', and even if they did, good luck in getting them to stay there. They also make great dens which can really benefit the settling-in period if they are covered with towels or a duvet, leaving access of course for the dog to get in and out if it needs a drink. You could also use this when toilet training, although, I say that tentatively as one of my rescues would even just go in the bed when it got too much to hold in overnight (not pleasant for you or more importantly the dog). When I got my first rescue, determined to raise her well, right from the start, I invested in a dog training company who assured me the payment was for a lifetime of support and would benefit us with an initial two hour training session. I didn't feel we needed to continue with training for long with our first rescue as it wasn't so much training she needed, more building up her trust, confidence and self-esteem. Nor did we need her with our second rescue, but thank goodness we had her there to call on when the two new dogs arrived. She was a godsend, truly, and such a comfort every step of the way until we resolved the problem. I highly recommend you invest in a professional to guide and support you with your new ex-street dog. Dog training classes are a great idea, but again the level of training you opt for is up to you, but just bear in mind that street dogs have wonderful and unique personalities that are a joy to behold should you care to look. Don't risk quashing the character before you've had a chance to truly meet him or her. You won't be sorry, I promise you that.

CHAPTER 8
MEET AND GREET: NEW BEGINNINGS

So you've come this far and now you're preparing for the meet and greet. All the preparations are done at home. The puppy pads are in place, you're prepared for every eventuality (you hope). The training crate is in place and kitted out like a real 'home from home' den (minus the mud and bugs) ready to aid a smooth settling-in period. Your vet appointment is booked, and the seat belt clip is in the car, so what next? You have your list of documents to collect and your contract to prove the dog is yours, along with your two leads (one with tag and details). There's a buzz of excitement and anxiety about what to expect. And then, suddenly after all the waiting and preparation, there they are standing in front of you looking all forlorn and bewildered, exhausted by the travel of the last however many days and unsure of their surroundings, sights and smells. The first thing that will hit you is how gorgeous they are and how clever you were in your choice. The second thing will be how coarse their coat feels. It takes a while for the coarseness to settle down but a good wash, regular grooming and a good diet will sort that out. Then you'll notice the smell, and, boy, do I mean *smell*. I advise you to secure your dog in for the ride home and keep the windows open in the car, regardless of the weather. He or she will absolutely stink to high heaven! Consider that they don't go through groomers before they travel, and having lived on the streets and in rubbish dumps and elsewhere (you name it), they are definitely eu de pong-ette! As bad as the smell is, try to put off bathing them in the first twenty four hours. Their smell is their identity and having lost everything else familiar to them, it's all they have left. So be kind and thoughtful to them. I'm not suggesting you tolerate the stench indefinitely, but just give them time. When you do get round to bathing them, take it slowly, calmly and quietly with the least amount of fuss and the most amount of reassurance. Read their body language at all times. If the ears go back and the teeth show, this is a good sign they are getting pretty scared and may attack out of fear. You should not continue alone if this is the case. Instead, get a friend in to support you through the process or you could invest in a muzzle for the dog before attempting again. Once the first bath is over, they will probably relax a bit. They just need to know that nothing bad is going to happen to them and having never been bathed before, the first time is pretty scary for some. With the bath done, next comes the grooming. Use slow, gentle movements until they are reassured that this new experience, this 'body massage' is actually a wonderful experience. Eventually you'll find your dog's favorite pose is on its back, legs in the air, smiley teeth with you massaging its tummy. You can expect to spend five hours plus in this position, as one of my friends found out when visiting a year after my first rescue. She was absolutely smitten with him and ensured he stay to deposit maximum tummy rubs. By the time he stood up to go, there was the biggest collection of hair and a thoroughly relaxed, nay, positively comatose pup. You may find the next week or so a little distanced. It can be quite worrying that they are so detached. After all, we know dogs to be full-on-fun but these dogs essentially suffer displacement. In humans, it is common and well documented that dissociation may occur as the result of a traumatic event. I see no reason why animals, (although not documented) are any different given the level of sentience they demonstrate. It is evident by their very behaviour that some form of dissociation behaviour does occur. They can go off their food, refuse to drink and want to sleep all the time. They can become detached or become erratic, flitting from one state to another.

It can be a very worrying time indeed, but have faith. Continue to offer food at regular times but don't leave the food down, especially if you have other animals. If the food goes missing you might think the dog has eaten it when really another animal has. The dog will begin eating all in good time. The main thing to ensure is that it is receiving fluids. Keep a water bowl full and try to encourage drinking. As long as the dog is taking in fluids there is less urgency for foods. Fluids ensure the kidneys continue to function and keep the dog hydrated. This is paramount. It may be a few days, or even a week or so, before the dog begins to eat and drink regularly but don't give up. In terms of interaction with the dog, aside from always offering water, allow the dog to come to you as much as possible and avoid getting in the dog's space. They are working you out and building trust with you from the moment they meet you. Keep it positive and reassuring for them. They need to feel safe and trust is a new concept for them. Always bear in mind that apart from the humans that rescued him/her, all previous experience with humans has not been favorable. I would start toilet training in the garden for the initial forty eight hours. Use your judgement. If the dog's eating and drinking well, then outdoor walks are fine (being mindful of skittish or heavy pulling behavior) but keep them relatively short and quiet while the dog adjusts to the new sights, sounds and smells. Always positively reinforce and remain mindful that the sounds of a truck thundering up the road, a car horn or stereo and even the sound of a screaming child may seem like nothing to you, but may be incredibly frightening to your new best friend. Find fairly quiet routes to begin with and gradually increase the busyness of the routes using your observation and careful judgement on how your dog is coping. Try to get into a routine as quickly as possible and maintain it. I found, with my dogs', they enjoy a routine. Anything out of the ordinary freaks them out. Another thing I discovered with my dogs' is that they like to be talked to. I'm not being anthropomorphic here. I'm serious. They love it when I converse with them or sing to them (at least someone appreciates my dulcet tones). The sound of my voice is soothing to them because it offers safety and security. Whenever anything happens out of the blue, or even if my male dog has found treasure in the form of an unguarded black sack of rubbish that hasn't yet made it outside, talking to him rather than yelling at him and ridiculing him works better. He may not understand what I'm saying bar a few familiar sounds, but you can be sure he's reading my body language always. He knows he shouldn't have done it, admits it was his guilty pleasure and skulks off to his bed to consider the delicious delicacies of cat candy (cat poop) and remnants of dinners for the last few days. Seriously, you can take the dog out of the street, but you can't take the street out of the dog. Talking to your dog is a good way of building trust. Keeping the tone kind and light, in your normal tone is a fabulous tool. I highly recommend more people talk to their dogs', cats', in fact, all companion animals.

One thing I haven't covered yet is other pets. Unless you've been told your dog is good with cats', assume it isn't, and even if you're told it is, assess the situation by keeping a collar and lead on your dog in the house for a few days. It's easier to grab a lead and defuse a situation than to chase after and grab an already frightened but excitable dog. If, like me, you have dogs' at home already, you should introduce new dogs' on neutral ground outside of the house and preferably away from the garden, but if the garden is your only option then you have little choice. Keep both dogs' on leads and enlist the help of a friend or neighbour with the introductions if there is no other family member. Again, keep your new dog on a lead when in the house for the first few days or at least gauge carefully the situation if you intend letting them off-lead around other animals. At night time, you should ensure the new dog is crated and covered to protect both your original dog/s and the new dog. And don't forget to reassure your already established pets. This is a big deal for them and a fine juggling act for you, as you take everyone into account. Be kind, consistent and positively reinforce and, best case scenario, you will find your settling in period will run smoothly and quickly with a minimum of incidents. However, you should also be aware that it may also end up worst-case scenario, but you have options and, sometimes the hardest decision to re-home is actually the best decision for all concerned.

CHAPTER 9
IF IT'S NOT HAPPY IT'S NOT THE END:
POTENTIAL PROBLEMS

As we move closer to the end of this valuable insight and education on what it means to offer up your home to a street dog, I wanted to discuss with you some potential problems you may find with your dog that they may NEVER overcome. But that doesn't mean it's not going to be a happy ending. It simply means you will need to expand your compassion and understanding and work with your dog every day for the rest of their life. After a month or two of working through all those issues to do with toileting, walking et cetera, you may find that some issues remain. For example, some of these dogs' have witnessed horrors unimaginable, they've been at the receiving end of brute force and beating sticks, slip ropes and fights with others for resources. While you've done everything in your power to treat your dog with love and respect, while you've taught them with kindness and compassion that humans can also be a joy and tremendous fun to be around, it is through no fault of your own that your dog may always have some psychological scarring. That's not to say they will have aggressive tendencies, although some might, while others may just let you know with a growl or a grunt if they've had enough. Remember there is a big difference between warning you and attacking you. Dogs will normally give plenty of warning if you are

annoying them in their space, it's up to you to read the signs
and not scold your dog but let it know you're backing off. I'm
not suggesting you let your dog boss you around; you have to
use your common sense and always put space between you and
a dog that is not happy with you in close vicinity. What I am
saying is that street dogs are usually quite tolerant, but if you're
in their face and they don't want you to be, they will grunt, give
a little growl, tense up and pull their face away from you. Read
the body language and if you're unsure what you're looking
for, get a behavioural book on dogs. I highly recommend you
invest in a dog crate or two for training and keep one for the
'den' (bed) and one for 'time-out' when training. I suggest two
because you don't want to associate the cosy den with being
in the wrong. The bed should be a place your dog feels at ease
to sleep in. It's your dog's 'safe space' and providing one will
support your dog mentally and emotionally. Essentially they
are just dogs but their circumstances have given them different
skill sets and finely-tuned senses.

One skill you may have an issue with is hunting. These dogs
have lived on the streets and are equipped to hunt. Hunting on
the streets is the difference between a meal and starving. Even
though you provide regular meals, instinctively your dog may
still want to hunt. It's not really common but it does happen.
I saw a post a woman made about her street rescue that was
out in the garden one minute and in the house munching on
a blue tit the next. Admittedly, not a very nice thing to have
in the house, and quite horrifying to discover, but just as some
cats are birders instinctively, so too are some dogs. That's not
to say you have to allow or encourage your dog to do this.
You can reduce the amount of times this happens by all the
same means you'd discourage a cat (collars with bells), but you
should expect that given the opportunity, your dog may well
want a fresher meal and will seize it if it shows itself. It's really

important you never yell or smack your dog for any reason and certainly not for this. Think of a habit you have that is not the best as far as other people are concerned- something like biting your nails, do you even realise you're doing it half the time? It's just something you do, right?! It's a tough habit to break, and it's the same for the dog except hunting has meant survival in the past.

Barking may be another issue (as I discovered with my second rescue). It was hard to even fathom why he was barking at first. He would just stand in my reception room and bark into the air whether we were there or not. And then I realised he was calling for his previous owners. He couldn't understand why he'd been passed on again and was calling out for them to hear him. It wasn't that I was mistreating him. On the contrary, it was simply that he just didn't know me. Everything around him was completely alien. It was an issue for me, I have to say. At first I was in despair, worrying about my neighbours complaining and that they would put in a complaint that would see him being seized by the authorities and goodness knows what happening to him. I contacted the charity about it but they didn't seem to have any solutions. I don't know how I got through it to be honest, but just getting down on the floor with him and sitting with him, talking to him and distracting him with toys seemed to do the trick eventually. Today, he is still vocal but usually it's through excitement of knowing a walk is coming or when he wants to play. He is less vocal and I am better equipped to quieten him down now, and he follows me everywhere. After forming a lovely close bond with your dog, you may discover that your dog develops separation anxiety and cries and howls for you when you go out. With regular dogs, you can combat this with regular short bursts out the door and return with lots of praise for quietness. I'm not entirely convinced this same trickery would work for a street dog as they tend to be quite savvy. By all means try, but it may be that you have to try a whole manner of distractions to keep your dog occupied or invest in a dog sitter. I am with my dogs all day, every day. They are rarely alone. The psychology is that your dog would rarely have been alone on the street. Even if it wasn't with anyone in particular, there would always have been people or other animals around. To then find yourself in one room, is hugely boring and lonely. They crave attention and for you that might mean a bit of a balancing act delivering.

Returning now to the topic of psychological scarring, I wanted to discuss with you the experience I had and, to some degree, continue to have with my first rescue. I ask you to bear in mind this is quite an extreme case and not all dogs coming out of kill shelters will be the same. Just like you and me, every one of them is different. My little dog was but around ten months old when she came to live with me. She was terrified of humans. To illustrate this, she would be standing on the floor looking around, I'd walk into the room and she'd hit the floor keeping her eye contact completely away from mine and wet herself. It didn't matter how quietly or gently I did this, no matter how much reassurance the response was always the same. This dog was severely traumatised. It was heart-breaking to witness and I felt lousy that I was somehow making this dog feel petrified. For months I just continued to gently talk to her, stroke her, let her come to me until eventually, she stopped cowering on the floor in a pool of her own urine. I have laminate flooring, which is a joy as it's so much easier to clean. Every day, as anyone who has laminate flooring will tell you, I have to sweep it over about three times - once in the morning, once in the afternoon and again at night. This is pretty straightforward, right?

Well, yes and no because while I enjoy a clean and tidy home, my first rescue is petrified of the broomstick or in fact any other household appliance. She either runs skittishly around the room trying to get away from me, or freezes and just wets herself anytime I come in the room with a broom. After five years and lots of reassurance, she is definitely better but she still won't stay in the room while I sweep…just in case. That is true psychological damage. How I manage it now is by respectfully calling her out of the room before I go in with the broom. She heads off to the back room or upstairs and remains nice and calm while I get on with the sweeping. Once done, she trundles back downstairs and comes to sit on my lap. Another issue she has is with certain parts of her body being touched. She is never aggressive, but if her ears are touched in a certain spot, if her ribs are touched in a certain place, or you touch her tail she screams and, I mean *screams*. It's not that she's hurting; she's had a full and thorough veterinary check-up and has a clean bill of health. These really are just all psychological scars from the time she spent in a high kill shelter before a brave rescuer bartered for her and took her to safety. The first few times it happened I felt awful, that I'd really hurt her somehow but, how did I hurt her? I just stroked her. Her scream is harrowing to hear and being a highly sensitive person, it set me on edge and hung with me for many days and in fact weeks after. So how do you manage something like that? Well, with time, care and respect. When it happens now, rather than pulling away from her in complete shock and horror which only makes her belief of violence more real, I stay and stroke her gently on another part of her body and tell her that I'm sorry, that I love her and she's ok. She then starts licking my hand as if to say, "I know you didn't mean it and I love you". And that is how we get through each and every day now. Some days are better than others but every day is worth it to be with her. Not all dogs have had such an extreme past, but even so, watching the mental scars play out from time to time is heart-breaking, when you know there is nothing you can physically do to really end those aches they feel in their heart or nightmares in their minds. Let me share with you my experience with abandonment and my second rescue. After the walking issues discussed in the last chapter were worked out, it became apparent that he would get incredibly excited every time he saw a truck. He would just launch himself towards the road (hence another reason for the short lead), jump about and then stand there with hope and expectation, waiting for the truck to stop and come and get him to take him *home*. And then with his physical body literally dropping in defeat and disappointment, all his excitement and expectation would just drip away and roll down the nearest drain. It seemed clear to me that despite his fiasco when first arriving in the UK, he must at some point have belonged to someone who owned a truck, my guess is a guy with a truck who, possibly, worked in the forest industry given his three favorite things are men, trucks and the forest. Three years on and still this little lad carries out the same routine every time he sees a truck coming down the road, his face lights up, his body becomes full of life and lifted with excitement and then it passes him. He leaps about as if to say "they came back for me, I knew they would" and then '*boom*', back to reality. It is heart-breaking to see and experience. I want to ease his pain in as many ways as I can, but this one is simply not possible. So how do I manage it? Well, I acknowledge it as it unfolds as no amount of distraction works for him. He is more focused than any dog I have ever seen when this happens. I then fuss him to convey that I understand what he's feeling and that I love him. We give each other a knowing look and walk on. Back home, he quenches his thirst after his walk, then hops up to sit with me and snuggles in as close as he can, giving a little grumble if I stop stroking and reassuring him. These are just a few issues based on my own experience. I'm sure there are hundreds and thousands more unique examples out there, but I hope these have given you some idea of how far that little thing affectionately known as TLC can go to make all the difference. Sure, you can treat the dog in the usual detached way that many see their dogs and hope for the best, but seriously, if you're not seeing your dog as part of your family, you're not the right person to own a dog, let alone a street dog. You see, in my experience of owning street dogs, they are without a doubt the most rewarding, loving and faithful dogs I have ever had the pleasure of meeting.

CHAPTER 10
FOREVER HOME

What does it mean to 'forever home' really? We hear it thrown around on social media all the time but I think it's one of those expressions that, while poignant enough, often loses its meaning. Does 'forever home' have a start date? Does it start once the initial settling-in issues are out of the way or is it from the moment you pick your dog up? Perhaps forever home is something that happens in your mind before it happens in reality, perhaps it happens from the moment you see your dog in that very first image as it was for me with all four of my wonderful canine friends. I have a wonderful relationship with both of my dogs', both are very different and each relationship is as rich and full as the next. They are not simply just '*the dogs*', they are part of my family, and as part of my family I include them in pretty much everything I do. I could not imagine my life without them, and thinking back over all the initial problems, it was absolutely worth it. Just as with anything, you only ever get back what you put in. So if you put in love, time and effort, you'll get back love, love and love. Street dog rescue is not something that is celebrated, in fact in some circles it's positively frowned upon and is, I suspect, the very reason you will rarely find any literature out there about it. While researching for this book, all I could find was sporadic research studies carried out by various well known charities (WSPCA in partnership with RSPCA and The Dogs Trust International).

These reports were more about looking at the size and scale of the problem rather than providing an insight to what it means to home one of these dogs. However, the information on the conditions a street dog deals with easily explains many of the issues they come with. While I understand the concerns of some groups who are against street dog rescue, through experience and education I passionately stand my ground and say, without hesitancy and, with conviction, that street dogs are the most loving, loyal and rewarding dogs I have *ever* met. They have given me some of the best and most rewarding years of my life. They are not like other dogs; there is something quite special about them. I have no doubt anyone who owns a street dog and shares a good relationship with them will support that statement. They have a certain feel about them that exudes gratitude. It's like you can almost feel the depths of thanks they have that is comparable to nothing else you've ever experienced. Once they trust, you can expect a tsunami of love from them. Investing compassion and empathy to make someone else's world that much better has been an incredibly humbling and thoroughly rewarding experience. Yes, the journey has been long, at times heart-breaking and extremely frustrating, but I am thankful for each experience. I hope you will go on to build a life equally as rewarding and full of purpose, and I hope you have found this book useful. While it may not have covered every eventuality (because who can know everything really?) I hope that if you go on to adopt your own fur babies from the streets, that you will forever love, trust and respect them. They will enrich your life in ways you never dreamed possible and they will fill your heart with so much love.

Life will never be the same.

REFERENCED

Beck, A. M. (2002). *Ecology of Stray Dogs: A study of free-ranging urban animals*. West Laffayette Indiana: Purdue University Press.

C. N. L. Macpherson, F. -X. (2000). *Dogs, Zoonoses, and Public Health*. Trowbridge: CABI Publishing.

Dogs Trust. (n.d.). *Dogs Trust Membership*. Retrieved May 01, 2017, from Dogs Trust: https://www.dogstrust.org.uk/get-involved/membership/

GFK UK Social Research. (2016). *STRAY DOGS SURVEY 2016*. London: Dogs Trust.

Gov.UK. (2017, April 26). *Bringing your pet dog, cat or ferret to the UK*. Retrieved April 29, 2017, from Gov.UK: https://www.gov.uk/take-pet-abroad/overview

Gov.UK. (2017, April 26). *Controlling your dog in public*. Retrieved May 01, 2017, from Gov.UK: https://www.gov.uk/control-dog-public/overview

Kathy Anzuino BVM&S, C. M. (Unknown). *'Street Dog' Polulation Control*. London: British Veterinary Association.

Kennel Club. (2017). *Pet Log*. Retrieved April 29, 2017, from Pet Microchipping: https://www.petlog.org.uk/

Mind. (2013). *Dissociative Disorders*. Retrieved May 04, 2017, from Mind - For better mental health: https://www.mind.org.uk/information-support/types-of-mental-health-problems/dissociative-disorders/

Mott, M. (2005, January 4). *Did Animals Sense Tsunami Was Coming?* Retrieved April 16, 2017, from National

Geographic News: http://news.nationalgeographic. com/news/2005/01/0104_050104_tsunami_animals. html

Tasker, L. (2007). *Stray Animal Control Practices Europe*. London: WSPA & RSPCA International.

The Kennel Club. (2017, February 2017). *Do you know dog law?* Retrieved May 01, 2017, from The Kennel Club: https://www.thekennelclub.org.uk/media/8277/law. pdf

RESOURCES

Bark Busters UK (Highly recommended Dog Trainers)

www.barkbusters.co.uk
Telephone: 0808 100 4071

The Dogs Trust
17 Wakley Street,
London, EC1V 7RQ

www.dogstrust.org.uk
(Look for your local branch online)

Head Office: 0207 837 0006

RSPCA

www.rspca.org.uk
The website will have information on your local office.
Click 'your local office' and enter your postcode.

Thank you!

As a thank you for buying this book and having learned much about street dogs, I'm sure you'll want to join me in celebrating not just street dogs, but dogs *everywhere*!

What better way to celebrate than a ramble with your four legged friend? Or, perhaps, your dog is a full on action pup? However you and your dog share the outdoors, I couldn't think of a better way to spend time together. To help you do that, I'd like to offer you 5% discount on your first order at 'The Fuzz'n Pup Inn Dog Emporium'.

Perhaps you don't have a dog? And maybe you don't know anyone who would loan you their dog? Well, I had considered that and, in our house, nobody gets left behind! So I'm making this gift available webstore wide! Why not settle down to some wonderful Youtube clips of dogs having fun with your favourite tea in hand! Choose from our lovely selection of premium teas at a fraction of the cost. So come visit us at: www.thefuzznpupinndogemporium.co.uk

T's&C's: Cannot be used in conjunction with any other offer. One offer per person. Offer valid until the 31ˢᵗ December 2018. Voucher Code: BOOKTFPI

Terms and conditions apply: Offer valid to one per customer. Cannot be used in conjunction with any other offer. Offer valid until 31ˢᵗ December 2018. Offer code BOOK1TFPI

Lightning Source UK Ltd.
Milton Keynes UK
UKOW04f1426290917
310133UK00001B/58/P